Praise for
Shaken

"Tim Tebow is not an athlete—*athlete* is what Tim fills in on his tax return. That does not begin to tell the story of who he is. Tim is a role model, an inspiration to those who have a dream and are willing to accept life as a journey full of ups and downs."

—JON BON JOVI, singer-songwriter

"*Shaken* shows us a side of Tim Tebow that we've never gotten to see before. In this book, Tim comes alongside his reader and says, 'I've been there too,' and proceeds to show us how God is faithful even when our entire lives feel shaken to the core."

—MARK BATTERSON, pastor and *New York Times* best-selling author of *The Circle Maker*

"Tim is a remarkable example of one who combines strength and boldness with kindness and compassion, and I'm always encouraged to hear of how he is using his tremendous platform to share the love and truth of our Lord with those who need it most."

—RAVI ZACHARIAS, apologist, author, and president of RZIM

"Tim has always inspired me with his dedication to grow and improve in all aspects of life, especially his faith. With this book, Tim encourages readers to keep moving and stay strong while battling life's obstacles."

—CAM NEWTON, quarterback for the Carolina Panthers

"Whether or not you've followed Tim's career, *Shaken* speaks to something we've all had to deal with—trusting God when the plans for our lives don't work out as we expected. Tim shares his journey from the Broncos to the Jets to the Patriots and beyond with refreshing honesty. He comes alongside us as a friend and gives us hope for the days our lives take an unexpected turn. I am so grateful to call Tim my friend; his life and passion constantly inspire me! Whatever Tim does he does with all his heart, and this book reflects that incredible commitment! I love Tim, and by the end of this book, you will too!"

—JUDAH SMITH, lead pastor of the City Church and *New York Times* best-selling author of *Jesus Is* _____.

"*Shaken* is everyone's story. All of us know what it is to experience the best of days and the lowest of days. For Tim, he's lived those days in public. I have the privilege to call Tim my friend and can tell you that with him, what you see is what you get, which seems rare these days! I appreciate how real and raw Tim is with his own struggles. In *Shaken* you will find great encouragement for your own life and faith."

—CHRIS TOMLIN, worship leader and songwriter

SHAKEN

YOUNG READER'S EDITION

Books by Tim Tebow

Through My Eyes

Shaken

Shaken Bible Study

Shaken Bible Study DVD

Know Who You Are. Live Like It Matters.

TIM TEBOW

WITH A.J. GREGORY

YOUNG READER'S EDITION

SHAKEN

FIGHTING TO STAND STRONG
NO MATTER WHAT COMES YOUR WAY

WATERBROOK

SHAKEN: YOUNG READER'S EDITION

Details in some anecdotes and stories have been changed to protect the identities of the persons involved.

This work is based on *Shaken* by Tim Tebow, first published in hardcover by WaterBrook in 2016. *Shaken* copyright © 2016 by Timothy R. Tebow.

Hardcover ISBN 978-0-7352-8996-3
eBook ISBN 978-0-7352-8997-0

Cover design by Kristopher K. Orr; cover photography by Bryan Soderlind

Library of Congress Cataloging-in-Publication Data
Names: Tebow, Tim, 1987– author.
Title: Shaken : fighting to stand strong no matter what comes your way/ Tim Tebow, with AJ Gregory.
Description: Young Reader's Edition. | Colorado Springs, Colorado : WaterBrook, 2017. | Includes bibliographical references and index.
Identifiers: LCCN 2017016085| ISBN 9780735289963 (hardcover : alk. paper) | ISBN 9780735289970 (electronic : alk. paper)
Subjects: LCSH: Identity (Psychology)—Religious aspects—Christianity. | Success—Religious aspects—Christianity. | Students—Religious life.
Classification: LCC BV4509.5 .T43 2017 | DDC 248.4—dc23 LC record available at https://lccn .loc.gov/2017016085

Printed in the United States of America
2017—First Edition

10 9 8 7 6 5 4 3 2 1

To the two best things in my life:

Jesus, the greatest gift I ever received.

My family. The thing about family is that
you don't get to pick them. But if I could,
I'd choose every one of you. I love you, Mom,
Dad, Christy, Katie, Robby, and Peter!

Contents

INTRODUCTION

'm grateful for the life experiences I've had—the good, the bad, and the ugly. Sure, I've had my ups and downs. As I've done things a little bit differently, the world has tried to force me onto a roller coaster of identities. It has tried to tell me who I am based on my circumstances.

Was my identity found in the highs when I won the Heisman Trophy or later when the Denver Broncos were making a playoff run? No. Was my identity found when, a year later, I was cut from the team? No.

When I'm on top of my game, it seems everyone loves and respects me. But when I'm at the bottom of the heap, I get criticized and torn down. You know what I've learned through all this? How important it is not to allow either the highs or the lows in life to determine who you are.

It's tempting to define ourselves or to measure our worth by what we see on the outside—by how we look, by how athletic we are, by how much money we have, by what others say about us. The list is long.

Think about this. Who are you when everything is going great—when you're acing your classes, when you're winning the games, when you're part of the "in" crowd, when your home life is picture perfect? Now, think about who you are when your world is shaken—when you're barely passing your exams, when you don't make the team, when your parents are fighting like crazy, when your boyfriend or girlfriend just broke up with you, when you just can't push that sadness away. Sometimes it takes a challenging time to really find out who you are.

> **Sometimes it takes a challenging time to really find out who you are.**

While many know about my career highs, few know the details about the lows. Like having to learn that God's plans are better and bigger than mine. Or feeling torn about the future. Or dealing with my dreams being shattered after getting cut from three NFL teams. I admit, writing this book hasn't been easy. It was tough to relive some painful moments. But I'm so grateful to share with you what I've learned: I've realized that who I am has nothing to do with wins or losses, praise or rejection. It has to do with whose I am—whom I belong to. Knowing this, I can live out what a king from ancient Israel wrote in Psalm 16:8:

> I have set the LORD continually before me;
> Because He is at my right hand, I will not be shaken.

In this book I share parts of my personal life and football journey in the NFL. But it's not just about my story. It's about the truth I've discovered along the way. This is what's important. And it's also about some amazing people I've been inspired by in life, as well as through the Tim Tebow Foundation's W15H (pronounced "wish") outreach program. I created W15H to help bring faith, hope, and love to those needing a brighter day in their darkest hour of need. Funny, the kids we serve have given those very things to me. While I wish I could tell you about every single child and family I've met who have inspired me, I'm excited to be able to share a few stories with you.

Here's what you can expect to find in this book. In the first seven chapters, I talk about some of the lows I've experienced and the lessons I've learned through that time. Like what it means to stay grounded in the face of doubt and fear, why others matter, and how God has created us to be unique, not "normal."

> I know that when I'm settled in my identity, I live at my best.

The last three chapters focus on how we can make a difference in our faith walk. Because life's not just about us, right? When we are grounded in whose we are, we not only can handle the storms that come but can also live bigger and influence others for God's greater plan. We can use our stories, our talents, and our willingness to help others in their own stories.

Look, I'm not perfect. I'm on a faith journey just like you are. I have good days. I have bad days. Sometimes I get it right. Other days I struggle. But I know that when I'm settled in my identity, I live at my best.

I pray that reading this book strengthens your faith, gives you hope, and shines light on your dark places. My prayer is that after reading this book, you can walk away inspired. That you'll be armed with courage, ready to tackle life and make a difference.

1

CUT

**We must accept finite disappointment,
but we must never lose infinite hope.**

—MARTIN LUTHER KING JR.

The locker room felt grim. You could just feel the tension. Guys stood in front of giant wooden lockers. On hooks and shoved in corners were more than just sweaty shorts and worn helmets. More than stuff. My New England Patriots teammates were staring at signs of shattered plans. Failure. Disappointment.

It was late August, time for roster cuts. NFL teams start out with ninety guys. By the end of the last week of the preseason, the number drops down to fifty-three. During those seven days, you can't help but feel on edge. Especially as you walk into the locker room after a workout and from the corner of your eye see a buddy that you trained and worked so hard with. Now he's glum, black trash bags in hand. It was like that all day.

One by one, a handful of my teammates started cleaning out their lockers. Told to go home. That it was over. Some masked the disappointment they felt. With others, it was written all over their faces.

On one hand, I was relieved. It wasn't me getting called into a conference room and then having to dump protein shakes, deodorant, and cleats into a noisy trash bag. On the other hand, I felt for these guys. They were my friends. And now, they weren't on the team anymore.

I remember clapping one guy on the shoulder and saying, "Hey, man. God's got a plan. He's got this." To another, I gave a bear hug, saying nothing.

As the day went on, I thought about my standing on the team. I felt like I had gotten more comfortable with my performance. We had just beaten the New York Giants 28–20 the night before, August 29, 2013. In this preseason finale, I had finished 6 of 11 in passing for 91 yards with two touchdowns. Yeah, maybe I didn't do my best, but I was just starting to click with the team.

And then, sucker punch.

It was my turn.

I didn't see it coming. Maybe because I was one of the last players to get cut.

I spent that Friday training in the Patriots facilities at Gillette Stadium. As I worked out, I felt a bit off. In the back of my mind, I was waiting for someone to pop his head into that room and call me into a meeting. But no one came. That helped to take some of the pressure off.

After my workout, I walked into the locker room. Seeing teammate after teammate getting released made me tense up again. I said goodbye to the guys while anxiously glancing over my shoulder. Waiting for something to happen. Maybe someone to call me into an office. Maybe a text. But nothing. A part of me began to think I was safe. I remember earlier that day talking to Robert Kraft, the owner of the Patriots. I liked and respected this man. He told me he was looking forward to seeing me at a barbeque he was hosting for the team the next day. I took his words as a good sign.

By the time I left the building, I felt okay. And I couldn't wait to hang out with my brother Robby and my longtime friends Bryan and Erik. I love these guys. We always have a ton of fun together.

To help distract me, the four of us hit a movie theater nearby. And after wasting an hour and a half of our lives watching a terribly boring flick, we parted ways. Erik and Bryan headed to the airport to fly home to Jacksonville as Robby and I headed back to the hotel room. By the time I went to bed, I still hadn't heard from Coach Bill Belichick or his staff.

I woke up the next morning thinking, *Phew! I made it!* Then, my phone beeped. A text message from Coach.

"Timmy, will you please come in?"

I stared at those six words for a minute. The feeling of security began to shatter.

I drove to the stadium, trying to not think so much. Whatever was going to happen was going to happen. It was that simple. But that didn't make it easy to accept.

I tried to focus as I pushed open the glass front doors. The place was practically empty. Most of the team was headed to or already at Mr. Kraft's barbeque, which I still had planned to attend. I kept calm as I walked down the gray hallway. My flip-flops flapped noisily on the tiled floor. When Coach Belichick's serious-faced assistant led me to the conference room, I knew. In an instant.

Enter the sucker punch.

The room was bare. Just a dark wooden rectangular table and a few chairs. There may have been a window or even a tap-dancing flamingo in the corner, but I wouldn't have noticed. My eyes were laser focused on the two men I was certain were going to change my future.

Their faces were matter-of-fact. No emotion.

Coach Belichick sat in a chair on the opposite side of the table. Coach Josh Mc-Daniels, who had drafted me to the Denver Broncos three and a half years earlier, stood in a nearby corner to his left. Someone waved his hand for me to sit. Their faces were matter-of-fact. No emotion.

While I can't remember who spoke first or what he said, I think Coach Belichick broke the silence by saying, "Good job on the last game, Timmy."

I nodded, staying quiet. My relationship with Coach Belichick had been good since my Gator days. He would watch me train, encourage me. I liked the guy. And I wanted to play for him. I wanted to work hard and prove I was the right choice.

"It's not the right fit," Coach Belichick said.

My stomach churned. I felt disappointed. I felt I had let myself down. I didn't believe I performed as well in practice or the preseason as I could have, but I was getting better. I had been stoked about getting to learn and train under Tom Brady, one of the best quarterbacks of all time. I planned on using that experience to become one of the best quarterbacks of all time, too. At the beginning of training camp, I put a lot of pressure on myself to be like Tom and train like Tom, but then I realized it wasn't about being Tom. It was about being me and doing my best. But all this didn't matter. My effort wasn't enough.

Honestly, it hurt. I had hoped Coaches Belichick and McDaniels would give me a chance. They were some of my biggest supporters. If they didn't believe in me, who would?

The meeting lasted ten, maybe fifteen minutes. I listened, not for a second taking my eyes off these two men. Though I felt they were sincere and truly sorry about letting me go, I didn't get any clear answers. They kept talking in circles.

As Coach Belichick said a few more things, I couldn't help but wonder, *Why wasn't I enough? Should I have trained differently? Should I have spent more time studying? Or more time throwing? Am I done for good?*

This wasn't the first time I was let go from an NFL team. In the spring of 2012, I was traded from the Broncos to the New York Jets. That move felt like a kind of betrayal. A year later, the Jets let me go. I didn't like this pattern.

As I nodded, still looking at these two men square in the eyes, I shifted my thoughts toward God. The One I believed had led me to

New England. *I thought this was going somewhere special! I thought this was a plan You designed for me. If that was true, then why, God, why is this thing crashing and burning?*

Then the meeting was over.

I gave Coach Belichick and Coach McDaniels hugs. I wished them and their families well. I genuinely meant what I said. I deeply respected these two men. They are great at what they do. And I didn't blame them in the least.

I blamed myself.

As I stepped out into the empty hallway that would lead me for the last time to the Patriots locker room and my very own black garbage bags, my heart sank. *You could have, you should have done more, Timmy. Why didn't you push harder? Train better? Work out longer?*

I pictured the thousands of letters, cards, and e-mails I had received from kids who looked up to me and had rooted for me. I had failed them. Again. I felt so embarrassed.

Thankfully the locker room was nearly empty, quiet. I grabbed a few garbage bags and stood in front of my locker, feeling like I was going to throw up. *Is this it? Will I ever wear an NFL uniform again?*

I stared at the bottles and jars of nutritional supplements that cluttered a shelf. Green fuel, protein shakes, vitamins, antioxidants— all the things that were supposed to help me get stronger, faster, better. *Dang,* I thought, *they were no help at all.*

I stared straight at the Patriots gear. A uniform I was proud to wear, that I'd never put on again. In a blur, I grabbed some of my personal stuff and chucked the items one by one into a trash bag. As I tossed in a pair of running shoes, I knew it wouldn't be long before millions of Americans would hear the news. I'd have to make a statement soon and wanted to do it right. I wanted to say—and mean it with all my heart—that I was grateful to God and to the Patriots for the opportunity.

In that moment, it wasn't easy. I knew God hadn't left me. I knew He still had a plan for my life. I knew He still had a purpose. And though my foundation in Him was solid, much of what rested on top of that was shaken. I love what boxer Mike Tyson said, something like "Everyone's got a plan until they get punched in the face." That's just what it felt like for me.

In that moment, it wasn't easy. I knew God hadn't left me.

A few teammates and coaches were there to say goodbye. They were nice and supportive, wishing me the best of luck. I can't tell you how much time had passed, but by the time I started filling my second garbage bag, I was over it. I took what I could and left the Patriots equipment in the locker. Then I walked out of the building, giving more hugs and saying thank-yous to the few people I passed on the way.

The summer sun felt warm on my face. The air was calm and still. Walking toward my rental SUV, which was parked in the middle of a lifeless parking lot, I remembered the last game I had played for the Broncos. On January 14, 2012, the Patriots killed us 45–10 in the second round of the AFC Championship playoffs. I didn't know it at the time, but during the game, I had broken my collarbone and second rib. As I climbed into the SUV, now a year and a half later, I slammed the door shut and thought, *This is the second time I'm leaving Gillette Stadium—broken.*

I sat for a minute, staring out the windshield. *Did that really just happen? God, I thought we were in this together! I thought we had a plan, a purpose! We were supposed to do some great things here!*

On and on these split-second thoughts blasted their way through my brain. Finally, I unfroze.

I picked up my phone and called my brother Robby, or my friend Erik, maybe both. I can't remember. But they kindly organized an immediate group call with my "circle of trust." My family (Mom and Dad, sisters Christy and Katie, brothers Robby and Peter) and a few close friends rounded out this amazing bunch. I needed their support, but I also wanted to tell those closest to me the news in one shot. I'm not a big fan of repeating myself, especially when it's bad news.

As I made the fifteen-minute drive through the back roads to the hotel, I told the people I love most that the Patriots let me go. They immediately began to encourage and pray for me.

"I'm so sorry, Timmy."

"This is not over."

"God's got a plan."

And then together, we worked our way through what I would post on social media. How do you respond publicly to such a personal loss? After much thought, I tweeted on August 31, 2013, 12:16 p.m.:

I would like to thank Mr. Kraft, Coach Belichick, Coach McDaniels and the entire Patriots organization for giving me the opportunity to be a part of such a classy organization. I pray for nothing but the best for you all. I will remain in relentless pursuit of continuing my lifelong dream of being an NFL quarterback. 2 Corinthians 12:9: "And He has said to me, 'My grace is sufficient for you, for power is perfected in weakness.' Most gladly, therefore, I will rather boast about my weaknesses, so that the power of Christ may dwell in me."

I was trying to mean every word. I really was. I knew in my heart it was true, but my emotions were working hard to get in the way of the truth.

———

That afternoon, I didn't have the heart to face a bunch of reporters or disappointed fans who were sure to flood the airport. So a friend kindly offered to send a private plane that was already nearby and fly me to Jacksonville. I planned to spend the rest of the day at Bryan's house with Robby. I had nowhere else to go. I'd been living in hotel rooms and rented apartments for the last few years. In fact, most of my stuff was in storage from the last cut.

Once at Bryan's, I knew I wouldn't be able to leave for a while. I'd be blasted by media and others about getting cut. People were already talking about it all over the Internet. Some offered support.

Others dished out hate. It seemed everyone had something to say. One sports commentator said I failed at a great opportunity. Another article said no NFL team wanted me. And then there were the thousands upon thousands of social media comments, tweets, and posts that followed each headline.

As I walked through the front door of Bryan's beautiful home, I remembered when I walked through these same doors in April 2010. The house was packed with family and close friends who munched on chicken fingers and mac and cheese while the seventy-fifth NFL draft blared on a large flat-screen TV. My brothers and I had watched the draft together at Bryan's house for years. This was the first time we were waiting to hear my name.

Moments before the start of my professional football career was announced to the world, I took a call in Bryan's home office. It was the Denver Broncos coach, Josh McDaniels. The team was about to choose me. A minute or two later, I became a Bronco.

Now three and a half years later, I walked into that same house. But everything was different. There was no party. No cheering. No high fives. And definitely no chicken fingers or mac and cheese.

I gave Bryan's wife a hug. She looked at me with tears in her eyes. Not knowing what else to say, she whispered in my ear, "We love you, Timmy." Bryan, Robby, and I crashed in Bryan's room. Remote control in hand, I flipped to the obvious choice—football. Watching the game, especially college football, brings me crazy joy. It's always been that way.

But that night, I realized my heart wasn't in it. It was the first and only time I couldn't stomach watching football. I'm sure it didn't help that during every game and on every sports channel, the news ticker kept running across the bottom of the screen like a broken record: "Tebow gets released from the Patriots."

"Hey, Bryan," I said. "Can you please find something else to watch?"

"Sure, man." He nodded knowingly and started channel surfing. Hundreds of shows and movies, and nothing to watch. First-world problems right there.

We finally settled on some movie. Though I tried not to think or replay the conversation with my former coaches a thousand times in my head, it was hard not to. My mind and heart were elsewhere. While the film ran on, and with Bryan to my right and Robby to my left, I struggled in my heart.

What do you do when your world is shaken? What do you do when your plans fall to pieces? What do you do when life is going in a direction you do not want it to go? Better yet, what do you hold on to? I knew in that moment, I had to hold on to truth. It was the only solid ground I had. I had to remember what God said.

And I would have to do this over and over and over again.

I brought to mind Bible verses that I was taught growing up and that I've held on to over the years. Like Jeremiah 29:11: "'For I know the plans I have for you,' says the LORD. 'They are plans for good and not for disaster, to give you a

What do you do when your world is shaken?

future and a hope'" (NLT). And Psalm 56:3: "When I am afraid, I will put my trust in You."

I remembered the things my mom had always said to encourage me when I was down, like "God has big plans for you, Timmy. Just wait on Him."

It was late when the movie ended. I'll never forget what happened when the ending credits rolled. Robby got up to return a phone call. Bryan got up to say good night to his wife. In other words, life was normal for them. Nothing had changed. But everything had for me.

I sat on the edge of the bed. As I watched Bryan's cockapoo run around in wild figure eights, it felt like my world had exploded.

What am I going to do? What am I going to be?

I don't put a lot of chips in different bags. I was committed to a career as a quarterback in the NFL. Period. End of story.

I prayed with a mix of faith and doubt weaving between my words. *God, I don't know what's happening. And I don't have a clue what You are doing. But I believe You have me here for a reason. I believe You've got a plan. I know this is not the end of my story. I may not be excited about what You have in mind, but I'm in this with You. Whatever happens, I'm in.*

Though I was disappointed, I was trying so hard to bulk up my confidence. Not in myself. Not in my athletic abilities. I was drawing inner strength in the One I belong to. In the One who created me. In the One who loves me beyond all love.

Sometime that night I got on the phone with one of my agents.

A few things happened when we talked. "Timmy, a bunch of teams are calling and hoping you'll play for them," he started, before rattling off the names of this one and that one. I was starting to get my hopes up.

My agent continued, "So this one wants you to play tight end. That one wants you as a halfback . . ." His voice trailed off. No mention of quarterback.

While every offer he told me about had really big selling points—and I was grateful for the offers—I wasn't crazy about any of them. Look, I wasn't being arrogant. I wanted to keep fighting for what I *was* crazy about. I wanted to fight for what I believed in. Since I was six years old, one of my dreams was to be an NFL quarterback. I didn't want to play professional football just to make a lot of money or to get famous. I wanted to pursue my passion of playing as a quarterback. To me, that was worth fighting for more than just making it in the NFL. I wanted to strive for my dream, not let others define me or my future.

My agent also gave me strict orders to lie low. The biggest distraction to being on a team is attracting a media circus, something I've been told I tend to do. This meant saying no to a lot of opportunities. Well, I wasn't going to sit around all day and do nothing.

I remembered Tom Brady once telling me about a guy named Tom House. House is a fierce trainer who tutors athletes on mechanics and also pitched in the baseball major leagues for eight years. I had met House before. The guy was nuts—in a good way. I knew I needed him.

Sometime before the call from my agent, and even during it, I made a choice not to quit. Not to complain. Not to let others define me. And not to stay stuck in disappointment or regret. Believe me when I tell you, I wanted to be angry! But I had to go back to the place of trusting God.

So I made the choice, on purpose, to put in the hard work of training while lying low. I was going to work with House, the best of the best. I knew my effort might not pay off in the way I wanted. I knew I might not make it in the NFL as a quarterback. But no one in the world was ever going to outwork me. I didn't know exactly what lay ahead, but I continually made the choice to trust God with the plan while doing

> **I continually made the choice to trust God with the plan while doing my part and putting in the work.**

my part and putting in the work. It wasn't easy. And I didn't necessarily feel good about it. But I did it.

I can't tell you how many people around me told me to take some time off. But taking a break wasn't in my vocabulary or my mind-set. Oh sure, in theory, it sounded awesome. I would have loved to rest and just hang out with my family. But instead of doing what I wanted to do, I chose to work. I chose to train. I chose to keep going. I chose to fight tooth and nail for my dream.

Two days after that call with my agent, I was in Los Angeles. I'd stay there for about eighteen months, training with Tom House at the University of Southern California. I'd live in someone's spare bedroom. I'd walk past people who would come up to me, with pity, and say, "I'm sorry." Others would simply ask for a picture or an autograph. And then there were those who would tell me their ideas of what I should have done or shouldn't have done and what I should do now with my life.

But I'm getting ahead of things.

That night, after Robby walked out to make a phone call and Bryan went to see his wife, and as I was fighting for my future, I couldn't avoid the ugly reality.

I had no job. No car. No home.

I'd let down the people who looked up to me.

No team wanted me to do something I'd dreamed of doing since I was a little boy.

What exactly did the future hold?

I didn't have a clue.

2

WHO AM I?

**There is no greater discovery than seeing
God as the author of your destiny.**

—RAVI ZACHARIAS

Being cut from the team hurt. No doubt, being told I couldn't do something I loved and was so passionate about—playing quarterback—left me shaken. Okay, so you may not have been cut from a professional sports team, but I bet you know what it feels like when life shakes you.

When you fail that big test . . .

When your best friend turns on you . . .

When that bully in school just won't leave you alone . . .

When your parents get divorced . . .

When you make a dumb mistake . . .

When it seems you can't overcome that learning or physical disability . . .

It's easy to question who we are in tough times. When my NFL career was crumbling, at times I'd wonder the same thing. *Am I the person who won the Heisman Trophy? Or am I a person who has been told over and over by so-called analysts that I can't throw?*

The dictionary defines *identity* as "the qualities, beliefs, etc., that make a particular person or group different from others." I like to say that identity doesn't come from who we are, but from *whose* we are.

My foundation for who I am is grounded in my faith. In a God who loves me. In a God who gives me purpose. In a God who sees the big picture. In a God who always has a greater plan.

LOVED BY LOVE

Who am I? I am a much-loved child of God. That's a big deal. It's important to take God's love personally. This may not be easy for you to do. Sure, God loves the world—we hear this all the time—but He also loves each one of us individually. With billions of people on the planet, I know it can be hard to grasp, to truly grasp, His personal love for us. But God cannot be measured. He has no limits. He can't spread Himself too thin. He generously shares His love with you and with me. And so, every single person on the planet is someone He made just to love.

Pretty incredible, right?

Love has been described as "the greatest and purest essence [nature] of who a person is."[1] God doesn't just choose to love. It's His nature. It's His essence. It's His being. "God is love."[2] Love motivates His every move. It's a reflection of His heart, of who He is. God was love even before creation, because He has always been part of an eternal community of love: the Father, the Son, and the Holy Spirit.

God's love is nothing like what we see acted out in the movies or even expressed in our lives. For most of us, love is something we *do* in order to *get*—what's in it for me? Or something we do to feel good—even though feelings can change in the blink of an eye. Or something that can be easily powered on or off, dialed up or down.

The opposite is true of God. His love is pure. It never fails. It is unconditional. It is eternal. It is not selfish. It is not out to get something. God loves because He is.

We can know we are special when we see the difference between God's love and human love. Coaches might love us because we score touchdowns. Teachers may love us because we ace tests. Your girlfriend or boyfriend might love you because you're cute or funny. Your friend might love you because you're always there for him or her. But would they die for you? Because that's what Jesus did. And He didn't just say He would die for us; He actually *did die*.

Jesus died for *you*. Did you get that? If you were the only person on this planet, He still would have died for you. That's some powerful stuff!

Knowing I am His much-loved child lays the groundwork for who I am. I am wanted. I am adopted into His family. I belong. A sense of belonging is a basic

> **My identity is based on belonging to God.**

human need, just like food and water. We all want to feel loved and accepted. But who I am is not based on what others think of me, what others say about me, or on fitting in with the "right" crowd. My identity is based on belonging to God.

There have been times when I was playing football that my

identity was muddled. But there have also been times when I felt so grounded in whose I was that nothing else mattered. I can say that when I'm clearheaded in my identity and not clouded by my successes, my failures, or the opinions of others, I live at my best.

If people like me, I will do my best to know whose I am. If people don't like me, I will still do my best to know whose I am. Whether I'm praised or criticized, popular or an outcast, have a little or a lot of money, I will always do my best to remember that I belong. That I am loved. That I am a child of God.

Trust me, when you know whose you are, it changes everything.

Stop and think for a moment. What defines you? What are you known for? Is it for how many people follow you on social media? How big your house is? Where you live? What sneakers you wear? Whom you hang out with? I can tell you that money comes and goes. Popularity, too.

I know failure is something that defines a lot of people. I could have easily allowed the lows in my life to define my identity. I've failed a lot of people. I've made a lot of mistakes. I've thought the wrong things. I've wondered how God could even use me. But just as I try not to let the trophies, the wins, the awards, or the magazine covers define me, I also try not to let the bottom points in my life tell me who I am. I just know that God is on my side. And with Him, all things are possible.

Because my identity is secure, I don't have to live up in the highs or down in the lows. No matter what happens, I can live with confidence knowing I'm on a solid foundation.

I've won two national championships and a Heisman Trophy, and I've been released from, oh, just a few NFL teams.

I've been praised by presidents, and I've also been shredded by the media.

I've been celebrated in rap songs and been the butt of jokes on TV shows.

And while I may get hurt, disappointed, or frustrated by negatives, my foundation doesn't have to change. I can hold on to God's truth. I know He's got a plan for me. And I know this is true even when I don't know what it is or when it looks totally different from what I imagined.

This is what identity is about.

Rock Star

Mark Stuart, lead singer for the rock band Audio Adrenaline, knows what it feels like to have your identity shaken by the unexpected. At their peak the band enjoyed great success.

Eight studio albums selling over three million copies.

Seventeen number-one radio hits.

Two Grammys, multiple Dove awards.

Artists don't usually end their careers when they're riding the wave of success. But for lead front-man Mark Stuart, he didn't have much of a choice. In 2004, while singing to a crowd of fans, Mark noticed something different with his voice. It didn't sound like it always had. Something was wrong.

At first he didn't do anything about it. Mark tried hiding it, writing songs so the band's guitarist could sing lead vocals. He also made jokes about sounding cooler as his voice got increasingly hoarse. But with each passing concert, Mark knew he had a serious problem.

For three years he saw doctor after doctor. Nobody could tell Mark why he was losing his voice. Specialists gave him shots just to get through his heavy touring schedule. Eventually the shots stopped working. Mark lost hope of ever getting his voice back. He admits that during this time, the joy of being on stage was fading. And then, people began to notice. He couldn't hide any longer.

Mark was finally diagnosed with spasmodic dysphonia, a permanent disorder where the muscles in the voice box suffer from spasms. He officially stepped down as the lead singer of Audio Adrenaline in 2006. No more singing. No more concerts. No more touring.

Despite having an amazing seventeen-year run with the band, the former rock star struggled at first to accept that he could no longer do what he was so passionate about. I mean, this was something he thought he was born to do. How would you feel?

Mark admits to feeling numb during this time. He admits to wondering, *What am I going to do?* He admits to feeling torn, sometimes accepting that God was in control and sometimes trying to play God and figure out how he himself could change his circumstances.

When I talked to Mark as I was working on this book, I was amazed to learn how grounded he has been for most of his life. He was the same person at the top of his music career as when he was a struggling musician. Mark's identity was still secure, seventeen years later, when he had to leave the band and say goodbye to something he had worked so hard to create.

"God was authoring a bigger picture," Mark told me. "He always gets you to where He wants you to be in spite of yourself."

I told Mark how much I loved their early hit "Big House," a song that described what heaven would be like. In fact, I got excited about heaven because of it. Even when I was a little boy, that song inspired me to do things for eternity, stuff that mattered.

And yeah, maybe a part of the reason I loved the song so much was because of the chorus, the part where Mark sang something about playing football up there. This catchy tune put Audio Adrenaline on the map. It was even named song of the decade.[3] What a lot of people don't know is that the tune was inspired by a children's song Mark heard while on a mission trip to Haiti.

Mark fell in love with Haiti as a teenager while his parents were serving as missionaries there. Throughout college and the early years of Audio Adrenaline, he regularly visited this country to serve with his family.

After the release of their hit song "Hands and Feet," Mark and the band felt called to do more than just sing about serving. They wanted to make a difference themselves. Moved by the growing number of orphans in Haiti, the band created the Hands and Feet Project. This organization helps keep families together and meet the needs of Haiti's orphaned and abandoned children. When Mark left the band, he devoted his life to care for those who are helpless. I admire this guy so much. He works hard to serve people and give them hope.

When I first met Mark, I was drawn to his vision for children with special needs. He told me that there are only a few orphanages in Haiti that take in kids with disabilities. Most of them don't even make it to one of those orphanages. It is a common belief in Haiti that babies who are born with special needs are cursed. The culture tells these babies they are not good enough, that they don't matter. Many of these children are abandoned at hospitals. Sometimes they are even thrown away in the trash. My foundation is now working with Mark's organization in Haiti to help build a medical clinic as well as a children's home that will help kids with special needs get adopted.

While he is no longer on a stage, Mark is still making a difference. And he's not bitter or angry, either. He told me, "God fills up so much of my life with good things that I don't miss what I don't have anymore."

Mark is often approached by people asking if they can pray for him. They also ask questions like "Do you want to be healed?" "Do you want your voice back?" and "Don't you want to sing again?"

The answer is always the same. "God has already healed me. I lost my voice as a singer so I can be a voice for these kids." Mark has not allowed the loss of his voice to define who he is. He is more than a rock star. More than a performer. More than a singer. He is fulfilling a greater purpose. He is part of a greater plan.

WHO'S ON YOUR TEAM?

On March 28, 1990, the Chicago Bulls traveled to Richfield Coliseum to play the Cleveland Cavaliers. The great Michael Jordan dominated. In overtime, he led his team to a hard-fought victory, 117–113. Jordan scored a career high of sixty-nine points in that game, making it one of his most legendary performances.

That night there was another, lesser-known player for the Bulls, rookie Stacey King. With a little more than six minutes left in the second half, King took two shots and missed each one. But on the second, he got fouled. Picture with me the scene. Imagine the stress King feels walking to the free-throw line. The crowd is going wild. All eyes are on him. Pressure's on. Beads of sweat drip down his cheek as he focuses, dribbling, getting ready to shoot. *I've got to do my part,* he thinks. *I've got to help my guys win this.*

He looks over and sees his teammate Michael Jordan, the best player in the NBA. Think King feels somewhat insecure? He shoots the ball. It flies toward the hoop, then clangs off the rim. Miss. He prepares for his second shot. Cavs fans are on their feet, arms waving in the air. More pressure. But this time the *swish* of the ball through the net echoes throughout the stadium. Score!

After the game, the press bombarded Michael Jordan in the locker room. As reporters crammed around the guy trying to get a quote, someone, probably a reporter who couldn't get close enough to Jordan, started talking to Stacey King and asking him questions.

At one point in the postgame wrap-up, King said, "I'll always re-member this as the night that Michael Jordan and I combined to score 70 points."[4]

That's pretty funny, considering King scored only one point. But in the big picture, who cares? The win was a combined effort. Michael Jordan was an extraordinary teammate to have. What would it be like to have him on your basketball team? Pretty awesome, right? It's practically impossible to lose!

Now imagine God being on your team. Imagine what's possible. Imagine what that could look like.

When *who* you are is grounded in *whose* you are, you realize it doesn't matter what life throws your way. When life starts to get tough, you can lean into Him for help. You can get through even the toughest of circumstances because God is on your side. He loves you more than you know. And He's got everything under control. He's got plans for you. Awesome plans! You and God are unstoppable!

You Have Purpose

God created you for a reason. He created you to be special. He cre-ated you for a purpose.

Purpose is one of those words people talk about so much that it's hard to know exactly what it means. Is it one big event that happens when you're at the right place at the right time? Is it doing something you are passionate about or are naturally good at? Is it doing some-thing that makes you happy? Does it have anything to do with helping others? While I'm not a pastor or a Bible expert and can't offer you a five-step plan to finding your purpose, I believe that it has to do with your identity.

A man named Paul, one of the earliest church missionaries, wrote, "For we are His workmanship, created in Christ Jesus for good works, which God prepared beforehand so that we would walk in them" (Ephesians 2:10).

The Greek word for "workmanship" is *poiema,* or "poem." Think about this. Before you were even born, God wrote a beautiful poem about your life. This masterpiece is about you doing not just ordinary or unimportant things but good works, wonderful things that make a difference. This means that you are important, significant. You matter!

When life gets hard, when someone says something mean about you on Facebook or Instagram or even to your face, when your parents are driving you crazy, when you're tempted to do something you know you shouldn't, when you feel pressured to look, act, or talk a certain way because everyone else is doing it, it's important to circle back to God's love. It's important to remember that He has an amazing purpose for your life. This is something I've needed to do over and over in order to encourage myself. Remember the last chapter? When no team wanted me as their quarterback, I had to keep reminding myself that God has a purpose. That He has a plan. Some days it was easy to believe. Other days it was a struggle.

I don't know what your purpose is. It might be to change the life of one person or one million. I just know that when your identity is grounded in God, you become part of a bigger picture. And you begin to live out this wonderful poem He has written for your life.

BUT . . .

You are unique. You are valuable. And you matter.

Do you find this hard to believe? I hope not. But if you do, I'd like to encourage you.

I can't tell you how many people I've met who struggle with doubt. Some have admitted to me that they feel they have nothing to offer because they're too young or not smart enough or talented enough.

Whatever you think you don't have enough of, know this: With Jesus, you have everything. With Him, you have what it takes to fulfill a purpose. You may not have graced the covers of fashion or sports magazines. You may not have a million dollars in the bank. You may not be Michael Jordan or Taylor Swift or Mother Teresa. But you have somebody. And with God, that's more than enough.

God is a big God. And He can do for you what He did for a little boy thousands of years ago.

You may have heard this story if you grew up in church, or this might be your first time reading about it. Whatever the case, it's one of my favorites. After a long day of sharing with many people the message of the Good News, Jesus and His disciples are ready for a break. So He takes them on a boat ride to the opposite side of the lake, where together they climb up a hill. I imagine they're all exhausted and looking forward to some downtime. But it quickly turns out that this is not going to be a time to recharge. The crowds come. And fast. It seems everyone in the village wants to get a piece of Jesus. The Bible tells us the disciples counted five thousand people that day, and that didn't include women and children. Some Bible experts say that would likely have doubled that number.

It's getting late. Close to dinnertime. Seeing the crowd, Jesus asks, "Where can we buy food to feed everyone?"[5] It's an interesting question, especially because there wasn't a supermarket around. Not to mention, Jesus and His crew couldn't afford to foot the bill for ten-thousand-plus meals.

And here is where it starts to get good.

MORE THAN ENOUGH

We don't know his name. We don't know how he managed to get the attention of one of Jesus's disciples. We don't know his story, his background, his education, or his family life. All we know is that a little boy in the crowd noticed a problem. And he gave what he had, his own meal, five loaves of bread and two fish, to help fix it.

I wonder if the kid wrestled with his decision to give what he had. Maybe he was embarrassed that he had so little to offer. Maybe he was afraid Jesus would make fun of him for it. I mean, really, what on earth can you do with five loaves of bread and two fish? I may not be a math expert, but I know how to divide. And five loaves and two fish do not make a meal for ten thousand people. It could be that he was shy, nervous. Maybe he thought the guy next to him would share his even bigger dinner. Or maybe, just maybe, the boy instantly felt moved in his heart to give. Maybe he knew that if anyone could do something with what little he had, Jesus could. Whatever the boy was thinking, he gave. And Jesus was glad to accept it.

"Tell everyone to sit down,"[6] Jesus says. Then he prays for the meal. I imagine it wouldn't have taken long for five loaves of bread and two fish to run out. But they never do. Not only does every single person on the hillside that day eat dinner, but there are twelve baskets full of leftovers.

Not just enough. More than enough.

I love this story because it reminds me how God can do a lot with what we think is a little. How He can take something that can be described as "insignificant" or "not enough" or "small" or "meaningless" and use it to perform a miracle. He can do the same with you.

It didn't matter if the boy had five loaves or five thousand loaves. The amount is not the point. God doesn't want your stuff. He wants your heart. Know this: it doesn't matter if you think it's not good enough.

No matter how many stupid things we've done, He doesn't look at us as stupid. No matter how many times we've messed up, He doesn't look at us as failures. No matter how many foolish things we've done, He doesn't look at us as fools. When we are willing to let God shape our identity, He will take whatever we have to offer and multiply it in ways and for a purpose that we cannot even begin to imagine.

So don't worry about what you don't have. Or the mistakes you've made. Take root in God. And watch as He unfolds a plan that has more love, more meaning, and more purpose than you could ever possibly imagine.

3

FACING THE GIANTS

Fear is a self-imposed prison
that will keep you from becoming
what God intends for you to be.
You *must* move against it with the
weapons of faith and love.

—RICK WARREN

n 2011, the Denver Broncos were earning the reputation of being a fourth-quarter-comeback team. I can tell you about game after game after game where the odds were stacked against us and winning looked impossible. But we never stopped believing we could win. And at the last possible moment, we pulled through.

Like when we faced the Miami Dolphins on October 23. It was my first game as a starter, and although I was giving my all, I believe I could have done better. On my first eleven drives, I was 4 for 14 for 40 yards passing and the team had zero touchdowns. And I was sacked seven times. With 5:23 on the clock, the Dolphins had a 15-point lead. (Did I mention they were 0–5?) We had 0 points. Pretty embarrassing.

But then we got the ball back.

Together my teammates and I moved the ball down the field with play after play and two touchdowns that finally tied the game and put us in overtime. We shut down the Dolphins with a field goal, 18–15. It was the largest deficit overcome in a victory with less than three minutes since the 1970 NFL-AFL merger.[1]

And then there was the game against the Chicago Bears on December 11 that same year. For just under one hour, the Bears had us in their pocket. I finished the first quarter 3 of 7 passing for 45 yards and one interception to Chicago's Charles Tillman. In the second quarter, I was 0 for 6. The third quarter was just as bad, 0 for 3. Not a very good start. And it wasn't looking like a good end to the game. By the time the fourth quarter rolled around, the Bears led 10–0.

With five minutes and fourteen seconds on the clock, it was turnaround time. Completing 9 of 14 passes for 85 yards, I led my team on a 7-play, 63-yard drive that Demaryius Thomas took home for a touchdown.

When the two-minute warning came, we were down by a field goal. With Chicago running out of bounds, and without any timeouts on our side, eventually I helped move the ball to a game-tying field goal with three seconds left. In overtime, Matt Prater took it home on a 51-yard kick to lead our team to a 13–10 win over the stunned Bears.

UNDER PRESSURE

Some people get better in the fourth quarter. Others don't. Pressure can paralyze, especially toward the end of a game when you're faced with the fact that winning, based on the statistics, does not seem likely. But those kinds of odds fire me up. I've always liked winning this way.

As a little boy, I never dreamed about winning football games 45–0. I dreamed about being down six points, crushing it in the last few minutes of the game, and then having a crazy celebration with my teammates afterward. Because that's what you remember in life—the special, unlikely moments, the comebacks, being dominated by pressure and overcoming.

What's pressure? Another word for fear. It's fear that tells us, *You're not good enough.* Pressure can overcome many athletes in big moments. It can be easy to yield to the fear and think, *I can't live up to the hype . . . I can't make this play in the crunch time . . . I can't perform under the bright lights when everyone is watching . . .*

Fear is a powerful emotion. It's something that controls a lot of people, not just athletes. It can push or motivate you to do things, sometimes even good things, but it will never take you as far as love can take you.

I think about my dad, a missionary. My father has more courage than anyone I've ever met. In 1985, he and my mom moved the family to the Philippines, an island country in the Pacific Ocean, to serve as missionaries. At that time they had nine-year-old Christy, seven-year-old Katie, four-year-old Robby, and one-year-old Peter.

My family lived on the remote southern island of Mindanao. Two years later they moved to Manila, where I was born. The government of the country was unstable. A lot of fights broke out between the Filipino leaders and the people who were against them. When I was only a week old, Dad watched, shocked, as armed rebel forces rolled down our street in military tanks. Chaos broke out in the city. Gunfire rained down. People were running this way and that, scared out of their minds. Needless to say, Dad came back quickly to our house. We gathered some personal belongings and left immediately for a safe hotel.

My mom recently told me that one time while Dad was preaching, someone with a knife ran right behind where he was standing, holding his arm high in the air as if to attack Dad with the weapon. My father didn't even notice the guy. It took only a few seconds before someone tackled the man with the knife.

> **God is perfect. His love is perfect. And God loves us perfectly.**

That's pretty scary stuff. My dad has countless stories of times he could have been afraid. But he wasn't. Why? Because he understood that God's perfect love for him is stronger than fear. First John 4:18 tells us, "There is no fear in love; but perfect love casts out fear." What does this mean?

God is perfect. His love is perfect. And God loves us perfectly. If we understand this truth, we realize that God is greater and more powerful than anything that might scare us.

Fear can keep us from doing things that God wants us to do. We might not share Jesus with a kid in the neighborhood because we're afraid she might think we're weird. We might not stand up for the kid who is being bullied because we're afraid of what the bully might do to us. We might not try out for the church play or the basketball team because we're afraid we're not good enough.

What fears overwhelm you? Are you afraid that others won't like you? Are you afraid of looking silly? Are you afraid you'll never fit in? Are you afraid you won't pass the test? Are you afraid you won't make friends at your new school? Are you afraid you'll never be good at anything? Are you afraid of making the wrong decision?

Now think about this. What are you feeding more—your fear or your trust in God? Do you keep thinking over and over about what you're afraid of? Or do you think about God's perfect love and the plan and purpose He has for your life? When you begin to understand that God's love for you is perfect, you can trust Him more easily. And if you can trust God, knowing He has a plan and purpose for your life, there is nothing you can't face.

LET LOVE RULE

Love is not a feeling. It's a choice. It doesn't say, "I love you because you will do this or that for me." The highest form of love is doing what's best for others, not ourselves.

In the New Testament, there are at least three different Greek words used for love. *Storge* is a natural affection we feel toward our family. *Phileo* is affection we show in close friendships. And *agape* is love that is selfless, sacrificial, ongoing, and unconditional. It's the love Jesus Christ has for His heavenly Father and for us. It's the highest and purest form of love.

When Jesus died for us, He showed agape love. Giving His life for us wasn't easy to do. In fact, on the night before He was to be crucified, He pleaded with God, His Father. While praying in the Garden of Gethsemane, He asked, "Father, if You are willing, remove this cup from Me."[2] It's pretty clear Jesus's heart was torn between doing what He knew was necessary and feeling the fear of what obeying would mean. Not only would He be tortured and killed, but the perfect relationship He had enjoyed with His heavenly Father would be broken. Being physically tortured is painful, to say the least. Being abandoned can hurt even more. But Jesus's prayer ended in obedience. "Yet not My will, but Yours be done."[3] *This is what needs to be done, so I'll do it.*

Fear doesn't make you give your life for someone else. Love does. So when you want to be the most powerful or the strongest, always choose love over fear.

THE FIGHTER

Prom. Graduation. College applications. Dates. Cars. Clothes. Just some of the things a typical high-school senior would be thinking about.

Except for Chelsie Watts.

In August 2011, after she had her appendix removed in an emergency surgery, this teenage girl was diagnosed with a cancer rare for someone her age. Instead of going to parties, hanging out with her friends at football games, and spending weekends at the mall or the movies, this girl went through chemotherapy and multiple surgeries. On July 5, 2012, Chelsie celebrated what she thought would be her last chemo treatment.

A year later, after she completed her freshman year at college, the cancer came back. This time, stronger than ever. With a quiet confidence and sweet spirit, Chelsie fought back. Though her body was weak and failing, her faith was strong. She held tight to her favorite verse, Psalm 27:1: "The LORD is my light and my salvation—whom shall I fear? The LORD is the stronghold of my life—of whom shall I be afraid?" (NIV).

By the time I met her in November 2014, she'd already had seven organs removed from her body. Despite being frail, she didn't come across as a victim of cancer. Always having a genuine smile, she came across as a fighter.

Chelsie and I shared an amazing time together. I was honored to have her pampered at a spa for a day and show her behind-the-scenes action at the sports TV show *SEC Nation*. I'll never forget how her face beamed while the crowd chanted her name after I introduced her to the fans at Texas A&M University. Not a dry eye that day.

Chelsie showed love and never-ending faith even when she was getting sicker. She told a reporter, "I know where I'm going to go. . . . I'm going to spend eternity in heaven without pain, without disease. And so I'm not scared."[4]

We kept in touch after that weekend. During our talks it quickly became clear that I wasn't the one encouraging Chelsie. She was always the one encouraging me. She was the one giving me the right perspective on life. Chelsie would always say, "God's got this." No matter what the medical reports said. No matter how many more surgeries or chemo sessions she had to go through. No matter what the doctors told her. No matter how weak she felt. She even wrote a song during this time. I love the chorus:

As the journey ended
I danced I learned I was healed
And if this should ever happen again I'll always know
When the road gets rough and it's gonna be hard ·
   Don't give up cuz God's Got This

That's Chelsie for you. Confident and unwavering.

I'll never forget the end of January 2015, right before Super Bowl weekend. I felt all out of sorts. I couldn't figure out what was wrong, but one thing was certain—I could not sleep. For three nights straight, I tossed and turned. On the fourth night, the phone rang. It was Brandi, a woman who works at our foundation and has one of the most beautiful and sweetest hearts of anyone I know. She told me Chelsie had taken a turn for the worst. My heart sank in that moment. I called her mom immediately. I am so grateful I was able to talk to Chelsie that night. And only an hour or two after I hung up the phone with her, she went to her heavenly home to be with Jesus.

My friend had fought the good fight. She had finished the race. She had kept the faith.[5]

Chelsie's mom calls her daughter a mighty warrior. And she's right. Chelsie was a warrior. How do you live in such a place of hope, love, trust? How do you keep from being overwhelmed by fear? How do you keep from letting the giants in life beat you down?

Faith.

Work It

The Bible tell us that "faith is the assurance of things hoped for, the conviction of things not seen."[6] I like what Martin Luther King Jr. said: "Faith is taking the first step even when you don't see the whole staircase."[7] This doesn't mean never worrying, never being afraid, sad, or disappointed. We're not robots. We're human beings.

Faith is not being overcome by the emotions we feel during our highs and lows. Instead, faith allows us to grow in the process. Though you might feel afraid, sad, or disappointed, faith helps you avoid staying stuck in that place.

Some might say that walking by faith is easy—or that it should be. It's not. Most things that are worth it aren't easy. Oh sure, think how easy it was for me to get super-pumped and put Bible verses on my eye black when I was winning championships and trophies and scoring touchdowns. It's easy to praise God when you're on top of your game. It's easy to praise God when you don't have any problems. It's easy to praise God when everyone likes you, when no one's fighting at home, when you're not being pressured to do the wrong thing. But when a giant stands in front of you—whether in the form of cancer or temptation or a bully—how deep is your faith then?

When I was cut from the Patriots, I had to remind myself over and over that God still has a plan. As much as it hurt and as hard as it was, I had to keep choosing to believe that His plan is better than my plan. That God is still God. That He, somehow and in some way, will come through.

A lot of what it means to work out your faith muscle is to choose to live above your feelings. It's about remembering that He is God and you are not. A friend of mine likes to say, "God is greater than your heart." It's easy to focus on feelings when we're sad, upset, or disappointed.

But God is greater than our hearts.

It's not that emotions won't get to us, or even get the best of us. Because when tough times come, we're going to get hurt and angry and upset. Think about it this way. Jesus had emotions, though He was always in control of them. He never let them get the best of Him. One time Jesus walked into the temple and was horrified to see it had been turned into what looked like a flea market. People were buying and selling animals. Business deals were taking place on tables set up in every corner. It was like a zoo in the middle of a bank. Jesus was so angry. He drove everyone out of the temple, turned over the tables, and ran the sheep and cows out using a whip.

What's my point? Feelings are normal. They come. They go. And they are constantly changing. We need to understand this and learn how to live above them, not by them. This means going deep with God. Growing closer in our relationship with Him. Praying and studying His Word regularly. Staying grounded in whose we are. And choosing to do what's right.

Listen, you're not always going to feel like doing the right thing. As an athlete, I don't always feel like waking up early in the morning to train, but I have to do it. We're not always going to feel like being kind to the kid next door who acts bratty. We're not always going to feel like loving someone who is selfish. We're not always going to feel like zipping it when we really want to cuss someone out.

But the more you make the choice to live above your feelings, to trust God instead of what you may feel like doing, the stronger your faith becomes. Like Chelsie did, choosing faith when facing a giant is what can turn you into a mighty warrior.

An Unlikely Soldier

Two nations. Two armies. Ready to fight.

The first army stands in battle formation, swords and shields in hand. Positioned on one side of a mountain, the soldiers stare into a valley that separates them from their enemy, the nation whose land they want to conquer. The second army is lined up on the opposite side. Thousands of soldiers are ready to defend their land.

The first army has guts. Heart. They have a well-organized military campaign. But their weapons aren't great.[8] That's just one disadvantage. There are more.

The second army is outfitted with experienced soldiers, top-notch gear, and impressive weapons. They have many reasons to be confident. Though they don't make a move, they are certain they will win. Besides their fierce iron weapons of war, they have a secret advantage guaranteed to crush anyone who dares to oppose them.

Somewhere from the back line, a massive soldier appears. This special-forces super monster machine towers over the entire army. He's covered in bronze armor, which cannot be penetrated even by the most skilled knife fighter. This dude is big and bad.

He thunders to the army on the other side of the valley, "Why do you come out and line up for battle? . . . Choose a man and have him come down to me. If he is able to fight and kill me, we will become your subjects; but if I overcome him and kill him, you will become our subjects and serve us. . . . This day I defy the ranks of Israel! Give me a man and let us fight each other."[9]

No one is willing to stand up to him. So every day for forty days, this gigantic commando comes on the scene in front of his army to yell and threaten and demand an opponent from the other side. And day after day, no one accepts the challenge.

Until God's answer to the giant shows up.

He's a teenager, fifteen or sixteen. The youngest of eight boys in his family. A red-haired runt who looks after his father's flocks of sheep. Tending to them in green pastures, he is responsible for protecting these animals and bringing them back home when ready.

One day this boy's father tells him to take some food to his three brothers, who are soldiers in that first army. "And bring back news of how they are doing, and how our army is looking."[10]

The boy nods and, at daybreak, rushes off. He finds his brothers in the battle line. They look worn, tired, defeated. Suddenly, a battle cry rings out in the valley. The soldiers assemble quickly into formation, weapons at their sides. The boy peers through the mass of men in front of him, looks across the valley, and sees Goliath, the Megatron of Bible times, blasting his way forward.

"Anyone today?" the giant roars. "Is there anyone brave enough to face me?"

Silence.

The boy elbows a soldier standing beside him and with his other hand points to the giant. "Who is this guy?" he asks, boldly. "And who on earth does he think he is?"[11]

The soldier gives the boy the rundown. He tells the kid that whoever ends up killing this bad dude will not only be a hero but will get a reward from the king himself.

Sounds like a good deal to me, thinks David.

Long story short, the little shepherd boy goes before the king and tells him he's up for the challenge. I'll bet the king tried so hard not to laugh when this rosy-cheeked runt stepped up. In his best trying-to-be-polite voice, he tells the kid to go home. But David is not one to back down. He gives the king a list of reasons why he's the man for the job. One of them is that in caring for the sheep, David's had to fight and kill lions and bears with a club and his bare hands.

What is a king to do? He says okay.

The king gives David his own suit of armor, which is way too big and looks absolutely ridiculous. And the king's sword and shield? They're so heavy the boy can barely pick them up, let alone fight with them. "No thanks," David says confidently. "I'm not used to all this stuff. I'll just use what I always use, my sling and my staff."

And off he goes. Stopping at a stream before heading to the front lines, David picks up five stones for his sling. He puts them in his pocket. Why five? As confident as this kid was, was he afraid that he wouldn't kill the commando on the first, second, or even third try? No. David knew Goliath had four family members who were just as big, strong, and dominating. If necessary, a stone for each bad boy. This kid had faith. He knew the kind of God he served. A big God. A God who makes big things possible. And he trusted that God had his back no matter what.

An Unlikely Victory

Cut to the battlefield. When David steps out into the valley, his country's army is cheering him on. They're also probably thinking he's nuts.

Goliath stomps in front of his own army's front lines. He looks at the kid with disgust, insulted by the obvious lack of competition. This is too easy. "Am I a dog, that you come at me with sticks?"[12] he shouts across the valley.

David is not moved by his enemy's terrifying appearance. He

doesn't see that the odds are against him. He doesn't care that no one believes in him. Standing firm in his faith, David replies to Goliath, "You come against me with sword and spear and javelin, but I come against you in the name of the LORD Almighty, the God of the armies of Israel, whom you have defied. This day the LORD will hand you over to me."[13]

David starts to sprint toward Megatron as the giant storms toward the boy, ready to crush the kid soldier with one slam of his monstrous foot. With sling in one hand, stone in another, David picks up the pace. Both armies clank their spears and swords on their shields. The rowdy chorus doesn't even match the roar that comes out of Goliath's mouth.

And then, legs pumping, arms raised, David lifts and twirls the sling. Aim. Fire.

While the second army gasps in horror, Goliath, blood gushing from the wound in the dead center of his forehead, collapses to the ground.

Game over.

How does a shepherd believe he can crush a giant? Where does he get such confidence? Was it skill? A ton of practice? The power of positive thinking? I'm sure his skill was part of it, but what gave David the courage was his deep faith. He lived it. While tending to the sheep in the fields, he developed his relationship with God. And as a result of working his faith out, David was able to push aside his fears and crush every giant in his path—the lion, the bear, and Goliath.

TAKE IT

I love what Jesus said in John 16:33: "Here on earth you will have many trials and sorrows. But take heart, because I have overcome the world" (NLT). What does it mean to take heart? Don't give up. Be encouraged. Lift your spirits. And do this on purpose. Literally, *take* courage. Choose it. When you feel tired, discouraged, or disappointed, make the choice to take heart.

Chelsie had to do this while fighting for her life. Do you think it was easy for her to take heart when she was sick and everyone else was out having a good time? I'm sure it wasn't. But she did. And look, I'm not telling you something I don't have to do myself. I haven't always taken heart every day, but I'm trying to live this way. When I'm tired, when I'm feeling unsure, and when headlines and critics tell me I'll never make it, I try to choose courage, again and again, to believe that God's got everything under control.

4

THE VOICES
OF NEGATIVITY

I like criticism. It makes you strong.

—LeBron James

When the plane landed at the Morristown Airport in New Jersey, I had a glimpse of what was to come. The media circus had arrived in town.

As I stepped onto the runway, a handful of people stood on the grassy areas near the Tarmac. They were waving wildly. A man reached out to take me to a waiting car. It was impossible to hear a word he was saying because of the two news helicopters that were hovering low, cameras pointing down in my direction. As we started driving out of the airport, more than a dozen reporters swarmed around the car, trying to ask questions. I was headed toward the New York Jets training facilities in Florham Park, a few miles down the road.

It was March 2012. I had just been traded from the Broncos to the Jets as a backup quarterback to Mark Sanchez. Playing for New York was like a double-edged sword. On the one hand, my agent repeatedly—and I mean repeatedly—told me to keep my head down.

Don't talk to reporters. Don't draw any attention your way. Just be a regular teammate.

Got it.

On the other hand, New York takes media coverage to a whole new level. It is, after all, known as the Capital of the World.

I was told that the next day I had to give a televised press conference where I'd be introduced by the Jets. I had never before heard about any backup quarterback in sports history doing that. Talk about weird. And talk about getting attention. I certainly didn't ask for a press conference, but it was part of the job. I couldn't say no. Over two hundred members of the press showed up. In fact, there was so much media that the conference had to be moved to the Jets' field house. All this to say, I wasn't quite sure how I was expected to stay out of the spotlight when it seemed others were pushing me toward it.

And that pretty much set the tone for my one-year season as a Jet. That whole year, I tried hard to be one of the guys. I wanted to hang out with some of my teammates after games and chow down some burgers without it being reported in some paper that I ate dinner at this or that restaurant and with whom. But it seemed everywhere I went, paparazzi followed. Cameras flashed in my face. Reporters spit-fired questions. Headlines blared—oh, I'll get there in a minute. And while my teammates were cool and I made some friends, it was tough. It was almost impossible to be "one of the guys."

Now, I might have been disappointed because I wasn't a starting quarterback, but I wasn't mad. I worked hard. I trained hard. I supported the team. I respected the leadership. And that whole year, I believed that eventually I was going to get my shot. I was reminded of what some of the coaches had told me repeatedly when I came on the team: "We are going to use your strengths, Timmy." "We are going to do this and that with you." It was exciting, knowing I was going to play. So at every practice and in every game, I did my best to be ready and waited for my chance. But the waiting only led to a chance that never came.

So, yeah, about those headlines. One reporter called me "the worst quarterback in the NFL."[1] Another said I was "the Kim Kardashian of sports."[2] Some called me inconsistent, others bashed me for my faith, and on and on. Though I was highly criticized in Denver, playing for the Broncos gave me the opportunity to shut down my critics. I could prove them wrong. I could play my heart out and do my best on the field. I could use the game as a way to dial down those negative voices. But since I didn't get a ton of playing time in New York, I didn't get that chance. And I was probably more tuned in to the negativity because of it.

During that time, I almost never watched TV or read blogs or browsed through social media. But I still couldn't help but hear about or see the headlines, the tweets, the magazine covers. Whether I was driving into the city, buying a cup of coffee, or just talking to someone, it was hard to miss. These stories seemed to find me everywhere I went.

One New York paper blared "God Help Him" on its front cover.

Another, "Holy Smoked." One paper wrote that an anonymous teammate said I was "terrible." The stream of negativity was nonstop. Though I tried hard not to let critics drag me down, it hurt coming from someone who was on my team, who was fighting the same fight.

Then there was the commentator who seemed to make it his mission to tear me down. His words didn't shock me. What did, however, was the handwritten letter he sent, apologizing. This man wrote that one day his kids had asked him why he was bashing me so hard. This struck a nerve, and he felt he needed to tell me he was sorry. He stopped criticizing me for a while. But then he started up again in full force.

Please hear my heart. I don't tell you this so you can feel sorry for me. I don't need or want pity. My point is you'll never silence the critics. I'm going to talk more about this later in this chapter, but for now understand that there will always be people in your life who will tell you you're not good enough. Some will say you'll never reach your dream or achieve your goal. Others will try to hold you back in some way.

> **What God knows about us is more important than what others think.**

Here's the good news. What God knows about us is more important than what others think. In these moments, we need to return to home base—we need to remember whose we are. We need to remember that the God of the universe created us. We need to remember that we are His workmanship. That He has a purpose and a plan for our lives. And that He loves us unconditionally, no matter what. This doesn't mean He loves everything we do, of course. He loves us despite what we do and the way we are.

We were created by Love, in love, and for love. When we understand this, it changes how we think of ourselves. We can hear negativity or criticism and it won't destroy our identity. We can be confident in who we are no matter what others say.

My time in New York was a lot harder than in Denver. As a Bronco, I was the talk of the town. I had some good friends. I lived in a beautiful gated community with basketball and tennis courts. Oh sure, I had my share of critics, but for the most part life was good.

While playing for the Jets, I moved into a smaller house in a little New Jersey town. Not that I needed a ton of space, but it was weird that my front door was only twelve feet away from the curb where TMZ and other media were parked. I even saw strangers picking through my trash six or seven times. What were they trying to find? I have no idea. But I did know that all this attention was happening way too close to where I lived.

Outside of practices and games, I stayed at home for the most part. My brother Robby was with me. While I was grateful for his company, we've never been the best at sharing feelings or touchy-feely stuff with each other. And without many friends in town and not being involved in a church community, I was lonely. Sure, I did keep to myself so I could stay under the radar. But still, it was a pretty dark place.

In January 2013 the Jets hired Marty Mornhinweg as their new offensive coordinator. I was excited about him coming on board. *I might get a fresh start, a chance. This might be my shot, my time to show my potential. I'm ready! I'm going to prove everyone wrong!*

I lasted two weeks into the off-season. Then, on April 29, 2013, I was released.

You already know what comes next. I was disappointed and, yeah, maybe even a little angry. I was also frustrated I wasn't cut earlier than I was. It would have been nice to have the time to get on another team. I was upset, but I also trusted that this was part of God's plan. It was a truth that I was having to remind myself of over and over.

And so I left New York and once again focused on training to get into the best shape possible.

When It Matters

Criticism hurts. It's hard to hear harsh words from a journalist you might never meet in person. It's harder to hear the same from a trusted friend. Let's pause for a minute. There are definitely times we need to listen and pay attention to things others say that we may not like. Not from Internet trolls or haters but from those who truly love us and know us best. I'm talking about a parent, a teacher, or a youth leader.

For example, if a coach advises you not to do something that might hurt you down the road, your best bet is to listen without getting defensive. Hard truth can sting, but it's better to deal with a bruised ego than a mistake you can't undo. Besides, those who know you best may see your circumstances a lot clearer than you can. We can all use some help with our blind spots.

A close friend may notice some bad habits that are dragging you down. A parent may notice how hanging out with someone in particular may be influencing you in a negative way. Proverbs 27:5–6 tells us, "An open rebuke is better than hidden love! Wounds from a sincere friend are better than many kisses from an enemy" (NLT). When others are challenging something you say or do, it's important to understand their character and figure out where they're coming from. Ask yourself, *Are they coming from a place of sincerity and love? Are they saying something that will benefit them in some way? Or are they truly looking out for my best interests?*

Sometimes hard truth needs to be told, whether we are doing the telling or someone else needs to tell us. When helpful advice or guidance is offered in love and comes from a genuine place, it can change our lives for the better.

I call these talks courageous conversations.

Look, none of us want to be judgmental. And nobody gets excited about having to tell a friend something that may initially hurt but might make the person better for it. I'm with you. I get it. I'm trying to get better about telling the truth in love. I've learned how important it is to affirm my love for a person before I tell them something that might be painful. We must let our love for others be the reason they listen and the truth be the reason they change. (In the same way, it will probably serve us well to listen to those who tell us hard things in this way.)

Now, let's get back to those naysayers, people who are critical and negative and who don't have your best interests at heart.

SHUT IT DOWN

Even when you are grounded in whose you are, it's not easy to hear others say bad things about you or make fun of you. If a Facebook troll, a school bully, or a frenemy tells you that you're dumb or ugly, or that you're too tall or too short, or that you dress weird or have a weird last name, or that there's no way you can do something you have set your heart on, don't get discouraged. Don't lose hope.

A promising star quarterback at an all-male boarding school had some big plans. He was athletic. Smart. Valuable. He had attracted attention from a ton of prestigious football programs around the country. Jacob knew what he wanted—to be in the NFL.

During a routine play in a scrimmage in August 2011, a defensive back crashed into Jacob's right knee. The talented athlete blacked out. When he awoke, he noticed his knee protruding to the side. *Guess I'm out for the season,* he thought while moaning in pain. Jacob was taken to the hospital. A paramedic suggested it was probably a dislocation injury. Not great, but something that would heal. And in due time, this high-school football player would likely be back running plays on the field.

What doctors discovered, however, was far worse. The main artery in Jacob's leg had been severed. He developed massive swelling that caused muscles and nerves to die. As a result, this young man's right leg had to be amputated just above the knee. Jacob was crushed.

After much physical therapy, he had to learn to walk using a prosthetic. And as he worked hard and got stronger, his desire to play football revived. It became something he wanted so badly. Not everyone thought he could do it. Jacob says that even "the doctors who I shared my goals with borderline laughed in my face. They told me it [playing football with one leg] had not been done before and that it was impossible. While it was discouraging to be shot down by professionals in the medical field, it also provided me with more passion and encouragement to prove those individuals wrong."

I met Jacob on Christmas Eve 2011 when I was playing for the Broncos. We've stayed in touch over the years. I've always admired this young man for his fierce determination. He never let others stop him from dreaming big. He returned to play ball his senior year of high school, completing the season with 12 of 15 passes for 141 yards and three touchdowns.

Not everyone rooted for Jacob. He says, "During the season I also had critics and individuals who were not so encouraging. Some of that came from behind my back from individuals who were around me every day. For instance, some teachers at my high school." Still, Jacob pressed on, building his confidence and working toward his dream.

And then he got a call from Mike London, the football coach at the University of Virginia, who offered him a preferred walk-on position. Of course Jacob said yes. In his own words, "There is nothing sweeter than proving doubters and critics wrong."

Jacob went on to graduate in May 2017 with a degree in foreign affairs from the University of Virginia. He will be moving to Los Angeles to help coach UCLA football's program.

The Negative Is Just Not Worth It

Criticism can at times be a bit painful for me to hear because I'm a people-pleaser by nature. I love to honor my coaches or a father figure and do my best to come through for that person. I love being able to do well alongside my teammates and crush it for them on the field. I like making people happy, whether that means making wishes come true through my foundation, killing it in a game, or doing something extra-special for my mom for no reason. But I've learned that if I'm motivated only by making others happy, by their approval or praise, there's still something missing.

While it makes you feel *good* to please people, it makes you feel *fulfilled* to please God.

There is nothing wrong with wanting to be the best or wanting to succeed. It's good to have passion and work hard. However, it can become a problem when wanting the praise or the success or the pat on the back becomes everything. Why? Because it doesn't last! In 2007, after winning the Heisman, I was told I was the best in the world. And then three years later, I was told I couldn't throw.

Another thing. When you work so hard to make others like you and make them happy, the criticism you receive hurts even more.

I wonder what side of the equation you're on. Maybe you've been hurt by something a friend or a bully said to you. Maybe you've been judged or looked down on. Maybe you've been sucker punched by a friend who failed to have your back in a situation. A negative word can hurt whenever it happens, but it's the worst when you don't see it coming.

And maybe, just maybe, you've said something mean, judgmental, or negative to someone else. Maybe you're the one who started that rumor, made that dig, or took that potshot. It is easy for me to remember times when others have hurt me with their criticism. It's harder to mention times I've hurt others with my words.

Several years back I distanced myself from one of my friends because he was involved with certain things I didn't support. Some of what I said to him may have come across as judgmental or as though I thought I was better than he was. I still regret my choice of words.

I don't know why it seems we are better at tearing others down than lifting them up or cheering them on. This reminds me of a story I heard. Put a bunch of crabs in a shallow bucket, and watch what happens. When a crab or two—the more adventurous ones—attempt to climb out, the others who are below them will reach out and pull them back down. The bottom crabs will keep doing this so that no crab will ever escape.

Okay, so you and I are not crabs! But sometimes we share that same way of thinking: *If I can't have something—that spot on the team, that cool boyfriend or girlfriend, the perfect family, the top score on the test—neither can you.* Sometimes when we're having a tough time in life, we want everyone else to suffer with us.

I don't know whether you are the one being made fun of or criticized or you've done your share of both. Either way, we need to stop being deceived by the negative words others say against us. And we need to stop saying negative things about others. When we are grounded in whose we are, we must focus on what God says or thinks about us, not on what others say or think.

OUR WORST CRITICS

Sometimes we are our own worst enemy. Consider what negative thoughts you've had about yourself in the last week, or even in the last twenty-four hours:

I'll never pass this class.

It's my fault my parents are having problems.

Why can't I be as (outgoing, artistic, good looking, smart, athletic —fill in the blank) as that kid?

I could never go to that school or play that game or be on that team.

I must be a loser if I can't fit in.

So many times we hold ourselves down. We compare ourselves with everyone else. And in our minds, in some way, we fall short. We're never enough. That person has it easier. She doesn't know what it's like to struggle with a learning disability. He doesn't know what it's like to be the outcast. The grass is always greener. In our minds at least.

When insecurities overwhelm us, we have to remember whose we are. It's pretty amazing how our identity lays the groundwork for everything! So remind yourself how much God loves you and that He has a unique purpose and plan for your life. And stop comparing yourself and your journey to someone else's.

Here's something to think about. Sometimes we can use times of insecurity as a challenge, to help us dig deeper and grow. Spend a few minutes thinking about something you can change. Like a bad habit or an attitude that needs tweaking. Maybe you go to bed too late. Maybe you talk back to your parents. Maybe you could treat your little brother or sister better. We can all change some things about ourselves. Me included!

When I was younger, I was arrogant. And over the years I have grown a ton in the humility department. I'm also a perfectionist. I'm always working hard to be the best. This is not necessarily a bad thing. But I've found that my drive can sometimes blind me to my current blessings. I have to work on finding a balance between trying to be the best at whatever it is I'm doing and being thankful in the moment for what I have.

If you need to make a change, start working on making that happen. One step at a time. Look, I know there is no such thing as an easy fix. Our problems don't get solved overnight. We don't be-come better people in twenty-four hours. Change takes time. And along the way, challenges will pop up. You'll even make mistakes. So you didn't spend enough time working on your science project and messed it up. Work hard, do more research, and crush it next year. So you made a bad play in the soccer game. Learn from your mistake, and don't let it happen again. So you fell into peer pressure and did something you shouldn't have done. Remember that Jesus forgives you, and use the experience to do the right thing next time. No matter how many times you get knocked down or mess up, you need to hold on to God's promises. You need to believe that He has a better plan.

Tough but Worth It

I know it's important to live up to our potential, to be the people God created us to be. I find that whenever I'm reminded of my identity, whenever I remember whose I am, I am more motivated to change. Because I don't want to stay the same. I want to be like Jesus. I want my life to matter. I want my love for God and for others to show in what I do and what I say.

We're never going to be perfect. But we can stretch and we can change.

When I was a kid, my life changed when I realized that working out made me faster and stronger. This was my first experience learning about the power of change. I became pretty freakish about the human body and what it's capable of. I begged my parents for weight equipment, anything that would help me become a better athlete.

And while Mom and Dad didn't have a ton of money, they provided what they could to encourage me to reach my goals. Dad even welded together equipment so I could weight train. It was creative and it worked! Knowing change was possible, I continued to work hard and get as fit as possible.

I love the saying "Hard work beats talent when talent doesn't work as hard." Someone might be better or stronger or more talented or more educated. But if we choose to put in the work of growth, we can perform at our best. And that's what matters.

If you look at successful people, I'll bet at some point they all struggled with self-doubt or discouragement or were just down in the dumps. But here's the thing: they didn't stay in that place. They made the choice to keep believing, to keep pressing on, to keep growing and changing.

> "Hard work beats talent when talent doesn't work as hard."

Growth is tough. It's painful. Do you know the only way to build muscle is to tear down the muscle fibers? This is what happens when you work out. And this process actually helps repair and strengthen the muscle.

Every day is an opportunity to grow, to do something different, to be better. You might have failed yesterday. That's okay. It's more important to get back up. To try again. To keep at it. Doing this while trusting God will help you battle the critics, the ones at school and the one inside you.

GOD'S GOT IT

We must cease striving and trust God
to provide what He thinks is best and in
whatever time He chooses to make it
available. But this kind of trusting
doesn't come naturally . . . we must
choose to exercise faith.

—CHARLES SWINDOLL

was an Eagle. Well, not technically. Two years had passed since getting cut from the Jets. Despite being out of the NFL during that time, I was in the best shape I'd ever been. And here I was, wearing the Philadelphia Eagles uniform, running plays and throwing passes during the preseason.

A few months earlier, in March 2015, I was in Boca Raton, Florida, exploring my next career steps. Offers were presented, some great, others entertaining. None ultimately were the best. I took time to think about a few, weighing the pros and cons. After all, for eighteen months, I hadn't gotten any calls to play as a quarterback.

As I started considering a few interesting options, Chip Kelly, the coach of the Philadelphia Eagles, called me. Would I consider playing for him? Um, yes, please! And the wheels started rolling to my becoming an Eagle. I was excited about working for Coach Kelly, and I thought the offense was perfect for me.

When I accepted the offer, I felt pumped. Surely God had brought this about. *This is it. This is what I've been waiting for! I'm supposed to be an Eagle.* I gave God an imaginary high five. Though this next step was quite surprising given the timing, I thought it was *the* moment I was destined for. And, oh, was I ready. The training I'd done with Tom House and others after getting cut from the Patriots was paying off. Of course this was divine intervention!

I was stronger. Faster. Better. In fact, the team handed out awards during the off-season, and I won the title for Big Skill, which was an award designated for fullbacks, running backs, linebackers, tight ends, and quarterbacks. My confidence was pretty high. *I'm ready. I'm going to be the best quarterback. And we're going to the Super Bowl.* If you don't know me by now, I like to dream big!

Getting another shot in the NFL was incredible. And it made me want to train even harder. As the preseason opened, I was excited. I had improved. And I showed signs of my potential during practices and games.

With four quarterbacks on the team at this point, one would have to go. I was gunning for the highest position I could get. During this time, the media tagged along on our journey. They were trying to figure out who was going to get cut. I didn't pay much attention. I just knew some people would root for me and others would hope I'd fail. No matter, I worked hard to win.

Right before we faced the New York Jets in our last preseason game, my phone blew up with messages. My family and close friends called and texted with words of support. They prayed for me. They shared inspirational Bible stories. And they took me down memory lane, telling me some of their funniest memories of me playing football.

I felt at peace. Content. I can honestly say I didn't have a feeling one way or the other of whether or not I'd get chosen for the team—and I was okay with that. I also was trying to seek what God wanted for my life. I was getting better at being more obedient to His guidance than clinging to my plans. Obviously, I wanted to be the quarterback for the Eagles. I'd be lying if I said I didn't. But I also knew the reality. The coaches were forming a fifty-three-man team. Maybe I'd be on it. Maybe I wouldn't.

Though we lost to the Jets that night 18–24, I was getting into a better rhythm with the offense. I felt good about my performance. Actually I felt really good. I threw two touchdown passes and had thirty-two rushing yards on four carries against the Jets. It wasn't the best, but it was good.

> **I tried to guard my heart. I reminded myself that I wasn't in control; God was.**

After I finished up with the press after the game, someone from the public-relations team said, "Dude, great job! I don't think you have anything to worry about."

I smiled. I was grateful for the kind words. Still, I was cautious. Considering the letdown with the Patriots two years earlier, and the Jets before that, I tried to guard my heart. I reminded myself that I wasn't in control; God was. And it wasn't my job to change His plan.

For hours, my phone buzzed with calls and texts from family, friends, and even acquaintances.

"Awesome game, Timmy!"

"You nailed it, buddy!"

"Proud of you!"

One of my agents called and said, "Great job, Timmy. I'm really feeling good about this!"

Sometime that night, one of the assistant coaches came up to me, hinting I'd be in Philadelphia for a long time. "Hey, Timmy," he said. "Have you bought a house yet? Where are you planning to live?"

Good signs, you'd think.

Before I left the stadium to head back to my hotel, I asked someone on the staff whether or not I should come in the next day. I was scheduled to fly out to Scottsdale, Arizona, in the morning. I had no problem postponing the trip for a day or so if necessary. Besides, if I was going to get cut, I wanted to be around to hear the news. The drama of getting released was getting old. I don't remember who it was, but someone told me, "Sure, Timmy. Why don't you come back, just in case."

So I did. On Friday, the morning after the last preseason game, I headed to the team's training facilities.

Déjà vu.

I trained. I showered. And I took my time doing these things. I wanted to give the people in charge every opportunity to find me if needed. I waited. And waited. And waited.

Nothing.

My friend Erik texted me during this time: "Are you doing all right? I know you have peace, but I also know waiting isn't that much fun ☺. 'It is God who arms me with strength and keeps my way secure' (Psalm 18:32, NIV 2011)."

"I'm doing real good," I replied. "God's got it."

I was on a plane headed to Scottsdale just before 4:00 p.m. that day, exactly twenty-four hours before the Eagles' deadline to make their final decisions. A flight attendant had just started to introduce herself and the captain, welcoming all passengers on board, when my phone lit up.

"Matt Barkley traded to Arizona Cardinals" blared an ESPN headline.

What? One of the quarterbacks I was competing against was taken out of the equation. This was a great sign. It meant I was likely going to make the team. I was pretty surprised, but for the most part I was calm. Collected. I had to be.

The news of the trade flooded that airplane space quickly. The flight attendant turned to me with a smile and said, "Congratulations, Tim!" Others around her in the first-class cabin did the same. Some of the passengers high-fived me, offering congratulations. Even the pilot popped his head in to see me. As hundreds of texts poured in at the news of the Barkley trade, all saying some form of "Congratulations," it felt a bit overwhelming.

In the past years, this hoopla would have been a high. At the time, though I was optimistic, I didn't jump to conclusions that I was an Eagle. And I felt more at peace with whatever would happen. Still, by this time, so many things were leading me to believe that I was meant to be an Eagle. The news of the Barkley trade seemed to be the clincher.

By the time I touched down in Arizona, no one from the Eagles had reached out to tell me I was cut. I slept really well that night.

At 10:00 a.m. Saturday morning, my phone rang.

It was Coach Kelly. *Sigh.*

I couldn't sit still for this conversation. I opened the door of my hotel room and started pacing the hallway as we talked. "We made the decision to let you go, Tim," Coach told me, as I took slow steps down the carpeted floor of the Fairmont Scottsdale Princess hotel. "I think you need more reps," he continued.

Disappointment set in, and frustration. A flashback of practices and games raced through my mind.

Didn't he see how much better I got? How much I improved? Didn't he see what happened, the touchdowns I scored, after I got my hands on the ball?

My plan broken. My dream jerked back again.

And as I walked slowly back into my room and sat on the edge of the hotel bed, I stared at the floor. My plan broken. My dream jerked back again. As peaceful as I had felt before this phone call, as much as I knew that God was still in control, I was hurt. Torn.

Did this really happen? Again?

Almost immediately after the call ended, sportswriter Adam Schefter broke the news on Twitter: "Eagles release QB Tim Tebow."

I quickly arranged a group call with my circle of trust. I was grateful for the support and encouragement my loved ones offered. I felt a strange mix of emotions. For the record, I wasn't happy. I was disappointed. A bit in shock. But as hard as it was to fight against my natural feeling to stay upset, I forced myself to stay with peace. I chose to hold on to my faith that God was in control, no matter what happened. Oh, I wasn't thrilled with the outcome. But I had to believe that God really, really, really had this. It wasn't easy, but I'll say the letdown wasn't as painful as being let go from the Patriots.

Later that day, Coach Kelly held a press conference where he broadcast his decision. In his words, "We felt Tim has progressed, but we didn't feel he was good enough to be the [No.] 3 right now."[1]

And still making the choice to trust God, I tweeted to the world, "Thanks @Eagles and Coach Kelly for giving me the opportunity to play the game I love! Romans 8:28 #Blessed."

Was I blessed? Yes. Did I necessarily believe it with every part of my being? I was trying. I really, really was. I made the choice—and kept making it—to trust God.

Got Doubt?

"I thought God had planned this."

"I thought He was the One who opened the door for me!"

"But I did everything I could! Why did this happen?"

Sometimes we can pray hard and believe God will do amazing things. Sometimes we're sure He's got a certain plan in mind for us. Sometimes, even while being faithful, a crisis hits us out of nowhere. And the doubts come.

It's what happens when you pray for months that God will keep your parents from getting divorced, but they do anyway.

It's what happens when you study for hours but still get a failing grade.

It's what happens when you do the right thing but get teased mercilessly because of it.

When life throws us curveballs, it's easy to allow doubt to creep in, no matter how strong our faith is. *Why me? Why now? Why?* We doubt ourselves. We doubt God's plan. We even doubt God. Why would He do something, or allow something to happen, that breaks our hearts?

Hey, I've doubted. I've asked many times, *God, where are You? I was depending on You. I thought You had this.* Sometimes I wonder if I wanted something so bad that I tried to make it happen on my own, only to fall flat on my face.

I can't tell you why bad things happen or why our dreams fail and plans shatter. It's a question that people have asked for centuries and are still trying to come up with answers for. This is something Job, a man in the Bible, struggled with. Though most of us haven't gone through nearly as much suffering as he did, most of us can relate to his questions.

Beyond the Doubt

Job is a righteous dude. He doesn't just go through the motions of worshiping God. He truly loves God. He is generous, kind, and faithful. He's the kind of guy you want to hang out with and even be like. Job is the richest guy in the neighborhood, but he's not obnoxious about it. He's a humble guy. He talks the talk and walks the walk.

One ordinary day, out of the blue, God and the devil have an interesting conversation about this man.

God is proud of His beloved child. "Have you noticed my friend Job?" he asks the devil. "There's no one quite like him—honest and true to his word, totally devoted to God and hating evil."[2] Job definitely gets a pat on the back, so to speak.

The devil rolls his eyes. "Gimme a break. The only reason Job is so faithful is because You give him everything. Who wouldn't sing Your praises if they had a huge house, a great job, and a wonderful family? The guy has it so easy!"[3]

After a dramatic pause, the devil continues. "Take it all away," he challenges God. "Take away everything good in Job's life. Then see what happens."[4] The bet seems an easy win.

Thing is, God knows this is not a bet. This is the story of one man's life—a man who loves God and who is loved by God. Because God knows everything, He already knew what the end result would be. This story was planned beforehand. Essentially, God played the devil into His own hands.

In a series of terrible happenings, Job loses everything. He loses his money. He loses his home. He even loses his children. Then he gets sick. His body is covered in painful boils. Not only is Job heartbroken, but he's also in great physical pain. One day his friends stop by for a visit. Though Job is hoping for an encouraging word or two, instead they try to figure out why their buddy is suffering so much.

"You must have done something wrong," they say. "It has to be your fault." (Hmm, it's so easy to point blame when you're not walking in someone else's shoes, isn't it?) Needless to say, these words don't help.

Job's wife isn't any better in the encouragement department. "Oh for Pete's sake," she groans. "Just curse God and die already."[5] In other words, give up. Call it a day.

But Job doesn't turn his back on God. He does, however, wrestle with doubt. He prays. He questions. *Why, God, why?* I love what he says at one point. "Though He slay me, I will hope in Him. Nevertheless I will argue my ways before Him."[6] *Even though my world is shaken, and even though I will ask why, I'm still going to trust You. I'm still going to put my hope in You.* Wow! I'm not sure I would have the guts to say that first part if I went through what Job did.

In response to Job's questions, God doesn't give him a list of reasons why he had to go through so much. Instead, He turns the whole thing around. "You ask me all these things, son. Well, it's your turn. I've got some questions for you." And in a beautiful speech that shows His power, His creative ability, and His all-knowing mind, God asks Job, "Where were you when I laid the foundation of the earth? Have you seen where darkness dwells and the way that leads to light? Do you know the path of the stars above? The workings of wisdom?"[7] On and on God questions Job about things so deep, the guy wouldn't even begin to know how to answer them.

It's important to note that God isn't shaming Job. He is telling him that there is purpose and meaning to everything He does. And though we may or may not know it in this life, there is a plan. We can doubt. We can question. We can wonder. But there always is a purpose.

Eventually Job's trials end. And God restores to Job even more than what he had before.

Why do bad things happen to us? Here's what I know: we are broken people living in a broken world. And because of our sin nature and free will, our freedom to make choices, bad things happen. Suffering exists. Remember Jesus's words to always "take courage" or "take heart"? Why did He say this? Because "here on earth you will have many trials and sorrows."[8] He was warning us that this life isn't going to be easy. There will be times when it gets really hard.

> **Though we may or may not know it in this life, there is a plan.**

Know that it's normal to doubt or have questions. God isn't scared of your questions. Bring them to Him. It's better to vent to

Him than to run from Him. But just as we must try to live above our feelings, we also must try to live above our doubts and questions.

If you're going through something hard right now—if you're struggling through schoolwork, having problems at home, or feeling depressed, or if you just can't take that mean kid in your neighborhood anymore, take heart. Don't give up. Keep trusting in God. He will come through in some way or another. Sometimes in the form of an answer to prayer. Other times He'll give you the grace and courage to go through tough things.

A Heart for Another

In December 2012, sixteen-year-old Garrett Leopold was in a Florida hospital, waiting for a heart. It would be his third one.

Garrett appeared healthy when he was born. Then, in less than twenty-four hours, his health began to fail. He was helicoptered immediately to a different hospital, where he was diagnosed with a condition called hypoplastic left heart syndrome. His heart's left ventricle had stopped growing while he was in his mother's womb, but no one knew it then. Without another heart, this baby wouldn't survive.

Garrett was only twelve weeks old when he had his first heart-transplant surgery. The next few years were full of doctor appointments, medications, and checkups. Through all this, he stayed relatively healthy.

After his first two weeks in kindergarten, Garrett started complaining about stomach pain. Turns out he had a rare form of cancer that sometimes develops after heart transplants. After four months of chemotherapy, including a three-month hospital stay, the cancer was gone. Since that time, however, Garrett had to visit the hospital every two months for treatments that doctors hoped would boost his immune system. In June 2012, Garrett had a heart biopsy. Bad news. His heart was failing. And he needed a new one.

I met Garrett for the first time while playing college ball. A friend had invited him to come into the locker room after the 2006 National Championship celebration to meet some of the players. He was such a sweet kid. Shy but full of life. I don't remember exactly when, but I do remember spending some time with Garrett at Shands Hospital before my foundation granted him a W15H in August 2012. He was pretty sick when I met him again while playing for the New York Jets. The foundation flew him and his family out to see our preseason game against the Philadelphia Eagles.

Less than a month later, Garrett was admitted to Shands Hospital. He was immediately put on the heart-transplant waiting list. My friend stayed there for six months connected to an IV and heart monitor. And he waited.

When the first week of March 2013 rolled around, Garrett's condition took a turn for the worse. On Friday evening, March 8, his parents got a call from the hospital. Come quick, they were told, you need to be here for your son.

Early Monday morning, at 3:23 a.m., a donor heart became

available. Sometimes when doctors aren't able to save a person's life, they can transplant that person's organs, like a heart or a liver, into someone who is sick to help save that life. Garrett's parents were overjoyed at the news but also felt heartbroken for the donor who lost his or her life. His mom said, "We never can say 'thank you' enough for such a gift."[9]

That Monday, Garrett had a new heart.

Though most organ donors are anonymous, it didn't take too long before both families began to realize a connection. Eighteen-year-old Amanda Pierce had been a senior in high school. At the same time Garrett started fighting for his life, Amanda was involved in a car accident. She passed away. Amanda's family found Garrett through social media. When they first reached out, Garrett wasn't ready to connect. He felt guilty about his new heart.

Finally, on March 9, one year after Amanda passed away, Garrett and his mom met Amanda's parents face to face. In a powerful and emotional meeting, Amanda's parents showed Garrett and his mom pictures of their beloved daughter. Tears were shed. Stories shared. Later, in an interview with local media, Amanda's mom said something I'll never forget: "There is no doubt in my mind that God intervened. This is tragic and awful and unspeakable, but it can at least still bring something miraculous from the tragedy."

Garrett recently said, "Amanda's parents are loving and always tell me I am worthy of Amanda's heart. We have met many times for dinner, concerts. Amanda's family is a part of my family. I am a junior at Mulberry High School, and some days are rough and some days are better. I feel really humbled and honored, also blessed, to say I received the gift of life through Amanda's heart. God has been good."

GOD WON'T WASTE YOUR PAIN

Not every prayer is answered the way we want. Sometimes things happen for reasons we can't explain, that don't make sense, or that seem unfair. If today you're going through a tough time, know that it's for a purpose. One of my favorite quotes is from my big sister Christy. In the midst of her struggles with health and the challenges of being a missionary overseas, she became convinced that "God will never waste pain that's offered to Him." I love that. God will never waste your pain. He will never waste your heartache.

The Bible tells us, "God causes all things to work together for good to those who love God, to those who are called according to His purpose."[10] If we let Him, God can use all things for good, even the bad.

I know it's easier to hold on to the bad stuff and keep God out of the picture. But when we do, we're the ones who suffer. We become bitter. And that bitterness can keep us from becoming the people God created us to be. Though it's not easy, we need to remember God has designed a huge and masterful plan. Something bigger than ourselves. A missionary named Paul said it this way: "Now we see in a mirror dimly, but then face to face; now I know in part, but then I will know fully."[11]

God's perspective is bigger than ours. He sees beyond today and even tomorrow.

Trust God. Trust His heart. Trust that He loves you. Trust that He has a plan. If you have to do this with doubt and a lot of questions at first, that's okay. It's at least one step in the right direction.

6

THE OTHERS

I would rather walk with a friend in the dark than walk alone in the light.

—HELEN KELLER

Getting to the remote village was an adventure—climbing a rocky mountain, getting scraped by prickly bushes, swatting away the gigantic mosquitoes. Definitely not a walk in the park. But whoever said my first mission trip to the Philippines was supposed to be easy?

I was fifteen years old, excited to do great things on the other side of the world. With Dad leading the charge, a group of us visited local hospitals, prisons, marketplaces, orphanages, and schools. We shared God's love with everyone we met. I had an awesome time meeting the people of this beautiful country and was blessed to love on them. And I'll never forget one remote village we visited that took us a good part of the day to reach.

We rode for a while in a rugged Jeep, bouncing in our seats on a steep and rocky dirt path. When the road stopped, we got out and finished our journey on foot. Our first order of business was climbing a mountain. Seriously, a mountain. We spent hours hiking a stony path surrounded by tropical trees, some sky high. My leg muscles ached. Sweat poured down my back as the sun scorched us. But it was just a part of the adventure. And I loved it!

The view at the top was incredible. A blanket colored by more shades of green than I'd ever seen in my life stretched out before my eyes. Well, I'm technically color-blind, but I'm pretty sure it was green, since I was looking at trees. Clouds dotted the blue sky so close it was as if I could reach out and touch them. Beautiful.

When we stepped into the village, locals immediately surrounded us. Their eyes were wide with curiosity. Most of them had never left the island or owned a television. So for many that day it was their first time seeing Americans. The Filipinos were especially curious about the girls in our group who had blond hair. Fascinated by the light color, they would reach out and pat them on their heads. Some even twirled pieces of their hair around their brown-skinned fingers.

As our group walked through the village, men, women, and children followed. Some of the adults kept their distance but continued to stare. The children couldn't come close enough. They bounced around us, laughing and chatting away in their language as if we were old friends. Some wore shirts and pants that were ripped, stained. Others didn't have shoes on. These kids didn't have much, but they were happy. You could see it on their faces.

With the help of some of the locals, we started gathering the people together for a meeting at the high school. "We have news to share with you," we said, "good news."

The tiny town shut down. People stopped what they were doing and took off to follow us. They wanted to hear what we had to say.

At least twelve hundred people gathered right outside the high school. The area was packed. All listened to our message of hope. That afternoon, it was my turn to speak, with the help of a translator. The people in the first row sat on the ground right at the tip of my boots. And if I leaned over just a foot or so, I could touch row seven.

Right before I started talking, something caught my attention. From the corner of my eye, I noticed three boys moving. As I began to share a message, I couldn't help but watch them from the corner of my eye. They were walking slowly, from one side to the other, around the back edge of the crowd. They would take a few steps together, stop and turn their heads to listen to what I was saying, move a few feet more, and stop again. It looked like they were hoping no one would notice. Then they cut behind a building and were gone.

> **Right before I started talking, something caught my attention.**

I was stunned. It seemed everyone in the village that day not only wanted to hear our message but wanted to get as close to us Americans as physically possible. So why did these three kids leave? And, I wondered, why did I notice? The crowd was so big I could have easily missed them. It seemed I was drawn to them.

As I talked about the love of God and the special plan He has for each of us, I couldn't get those three boys off my mind. *I have to find them. I have to talk to them.* I ended my message with an invitation for those who wanted to ask Jesus into their hearts. I prayed with the folks who raised their hands and then thanked everyone for allowing us to be there and share with them. While walking away from the makeshift platform, mobbed on every side, I said, "God bless you," and gave as many hugs as I possibly could. All the while, I scanned the area left and right. I was hoping to catch a glimpse of those three kids.

As I turned the corner behind the school building, I noticed a bamboo hut. Then a head with a mop of dark hair peered out of an opening. A boy walked out of the hut, smiling. *Score!* He was one of the three.

I waved and said, "Hi there! I'm Timmy!" with a big smile. I invited him to come toward me. The boy didn't say anything but started walking my way. When he was close enough, he reached out his little hand. Wrapping his fingers around two of mine, he led me toward the bamboo hut where, I imagined, his two buddies were. Although I was a total stranger, he seemed comfortable around me. Like I was a friend. And I couldn't help but see something special in him.

I crawled inside the hut. Immediately I noticed one boy lying on a cot. The other sat beside him with his legs crossed and his hand resting on his friend's arm in a comforting manner. The boy who brought me in sat down on the opposite side of the one lying down. He put his hand on his friend's shoulder. They were all smiling, but nobody said a word. Just three pairs of eyes staring at me.

Still on my knees, I looked over to the boy stretched out on the cot and introduced myself. I was going to ask if they wanted to shoot some hoops or something. When I took my eyes off the boy's face, I noticed why he was lying down. His feet were on backward.

My heart fell. Fighting back tears, I felt small in that moment. I wanted to help him, to do something. I asked them their names, how old they were, and other things. Finally, the quiet broke. They started rattling off answers in broken English. It seemed they couldn't talk fast enough. After a few minutes I said, "I saw you guys while I was speaking. Why did you leave?"

> My heart fell. Fighting back tears, I felt small in that moment.

Sherwin, the boy on the cot, answered. "Our school principal wanted to impress the Americans." He paused, looking down at his legs. As his eyes filled with sadness, he said, almost in a whisper, "And the principal said that I'm not very impressive."

My heart broke more. This boy should have been the first one seated in the first row. This boy should be loved, encouraged—not ignored or treated like he wasn't good enough. In spending a few precious minutes with these three boys, I shared with them the love of Jesus. I told them that God had a special plan for them. I thanked the two boys for being awesome friends. And I told Sherwin that God created him perfect and that God thought he was very, very impressive.

Suddenly, I heard a group of people carrying on outside the hut. My team was preparing to leave and was looking for me.

"I'm sorry," I said to Sherwin and his friends. "I have to go."

"Can you at least carry me out?" Sherwin asked.

"Of course!" I picked the boy up and told his friends to follow. They walked on either side of me. One held Sherwin's hand. The other held his backward foot. Together we headed toward where our team had gathered and was preparing to leave.

And then, just before we said goodbye, the boys told me they wanted to trust Jesus and invite Him into their hearts. It was a beautiful moment. Three friends together accepted the gospel of hope.

I looked at Sherwin before handing him over to his two pals. All four of us had tears in our eyes. "I can't wait to see you in heaven, buddy," I told him, ruffling his thick dark hair with my hand.

He looked at me with a smile, his eyes sparkling. "Timmy, I can't wait to run with you in heaven."

In that moment, something struck me. I realized after meeting Sherwin that while I wanted to be the best quarterback in the world, I also wanted to change people's lives. I wanted to bring faith, hope, and love to those needing a brighter day in their darkest hour of need. I wanted to fight for those who couldn't fight for themselves. I wanted to fight for Sherwin. I wanted to fight for people like him. And as I stood on top of that mountain, the vision for a nonprofit organization—which we later created and named the Tim Tebow Foundation—began. Inspired by these boys, I pictured in my mind someone holding the hand of a hurting child and another getting help. For this is what Sherwin's two friends did. One stayed behind to comfort him, and the other, it seemed, went out to look for me.

FRIENDS MATTER

Not that I'm comparing myself to Michael Jordan, but stay with me for a minute. Imagine you're a die-hard Michael Jordan fan (this might be true for you). Say he was coming to your school to host a slam-dunk competition. Can you imagine having to stay back with your friend who just broke his leg? Would you be so quick to say "no thanks" to this amazing, once-in-a-lifetime opportunity just because your friend couldn't go? Don't hate me for this, but in my younger years, I likely would have left my friend in a heartbeat. "I hope you feel better, but I gotta go and meet Michael Jordan! God bless you, buddy!"

But not these two friends of Sherwin.

Think about it. These guys had never before seen visitors in their entire life, let alone Americans who came to bring a message of hope and love to their village. But they were committed to Sherwin, determined to stay by his side. They were compassionate and cared more for him than for these visitors to their village. Seeing how willing they were to stick with their friend, no matter what, changed my life.

We need to be like these two friends. When someone is hurting, sick, feeling blue, or going through a rough time, we need to reach out to them. Check in on them. Pray for them. Listen to them.

We need one another. God is a relational God. He designed us to be in community. He designed us to live in relationship with Him first and foremost, and then with others. This is what the church is supposed to be. It's not about four walls and a pretty building. It's about the people we do life with. We need friends who are going to have our backs. We need friends who can carry us when we're weak. We need friends we can count on. We need friends who will tell us the truth in love. I love this verse: "A person standing alone can be attacked and defeated, but two can stand back-to-back and conquer. Three are even better, for a triple-braided cord is not easily broken."[1] This is God's reminder that we are not meant to do life alone.

I remember right after I graduated from college, getting ready to turn pro, my friend Kevin, who was still in school, called me after he got out of class. He seemed pretty shaken up. Almost like he had been crying.

"What's going on, bro?" I asked.

Kevin told me he was so angry because one of his classmates had said a bunch of terrible things about me. "It took everything not to punch this guy in the face," he told me, still fuming. We talked more. By the time we hung up, I realized that this was a friend who would always have my back. Kevin was loyal and he cared for me, "a friend who sticks closer than a brother."[2]

When I was released from the Patriots, the encouraging and supportive words my loved ones gave meant the world to me. I'll never forget what they said: "We love you. It doesn't matter if you play for another team or if you never play at all. You are still and will always be Timmy to us, and we will always love you."

When I was having a rough time in New York, I cherished the weekend visits from my friends Brad, Kevin, and others. Most times we wouldn't do much except hang out, watch movies, and play video games. The most important thing was just being with them, laughing and goofing off with the guys who loved me for me, not for football. And when I was cut from the Jets they, and others, encouraged me to be patient. "Your time is going to come," they said. "Don't doubt yourself. You can do this. Just keep trusting God."

I am so grateful for the friends in my life. They love me for who I am, not what I do. They also understand me enough to tell me the truth in love. I'm a pretty competitive guy. Sometimes I want to win so badly, whether a game or a debate, that I end up hurting someone's feelings without meaning to. I can't tell you how many times I've played the game Mafia with my siblings or a Madden video game with my friends, only to watch the person I'm playing with stand up and walk out of the room because my competitive attitude got in the way of having a good time. Understanding this, my friends often know exactly when to tell me to cool it or back down.

> I am so grateful for the friends in my life. They love me for who I am, not what I do.

"No man is an island" is the famous line written by the poet John Donne. Funny, when life gets tough, sometimes all we want is to be alone. We say things like "I don't need anyone" or "I can get through this by myself."

I mentioned earlier how I was lonely during my time as a New York Jet. While one reason I kept to myself was to avoid the media, a part of me believed I could handle life on my own. *I'm going to be strong, push through, and fight my pain.* You know what I didn't realize at the time? That I needed others. That I needed support, even if just a few people.

Charles Dickens wrote, "No one is useless in this world who lightens the burdens of another." Friends can encourage us. Motivate us. Inspire us. Celebrate with us. Listen to us. Make us laugh. Offer a new perspective. Hold us accountable. True friendship is about trust, being open and honest, sharing, not shutting down because of pride. It's about believing with others. Loving them. Encouraging them.

If you're going through a tough time, it's important to lean on others for support, love, wisdom, and encouragement. I've had to do this often in my career lows, and I'm grateful for that support system.

WHAT WE CAN DO

Let's flip the switch for a minute. Ever get so stuck on yourself and your problems that that's all you see? You lose perspective. You forget about those around you. Sometimes we just need to take a minute and stop. Step outside ourselves. Pay attention to the world around us. And do something, no matter how small, to help someone else.

I think about being cut so many times and not continuing to live my dream of being a quarterback in the NFL. I could have gotten stuck feeling sorry for myself. And sometimes I did. But in the big picture, it almost seems silly. Who cares that my dream of playing quarterback wasn't being fulfilled? You know what thousands upon thousands of children all over the world dream about? Getting a new pair of flip-flops. Flip-flops! Do you know how many pairs I own?

Perspective.

It's amazing what happens when we think of others instead of ourselves or help someone when we're feeling helpless. This doesn't have to be some big task. You don't have to save the world. You don't have to raise a million dollars. You don't have to go on a mission trip next week. (Although I will always recommend going on mission trips!)

Think simple. Send an encouraging text to a friend. Make a card for someone who is sick. Instead of blabbing on and on about your problems, find out what another person is going through. Pray for someone.

You know what's so awesome about thinking about others instead of focusing on ourselves all the time? It's actually good for us. Research shows that helping others can help ourselves. It'll help us feel better, less stressed.[3]

Ralph Waldo Emerson said, "The purpose of life is not to be happy. It is to be useful, to be honorable, to be compassionate, to have it make some difference that you have lived and lived well."[4] We do this by reaching out to others. And we do this by finding a need, however small, and filling it. (More on this in the last three chapters.)

Who's in Your Circle?

You've already read about how I reached out to my circle of trust when I was cut from the Patriots, the Jets, and the Eagles. But I depend on this tight-knit bunch of family and close friends for more than just being encouraged. They help me when I'm stuck on a decision. And they tell me the truth, even if I don't want to hear it.

I think about the opportunity I had to host a TV show. It was a great gig that would last only a few days and pay a great chunk of money. I talked to my circle of trust. After each person on the line shared his or her thoughts, we all agreed that it was a good thing. Easy decision, right? The problem was, I later found out that I'd previously committed to an event on one of the days I would be filming for this show.

One of my agents, who was pushing me to say yes, told me, "Just don't show up to the event."

I couldn't believe he'd said that. "Are you kidding me? These people are counting on me!"

I knew my answer. I couldn't just back out. And I definitely wasn't going to not show up.

Though my agent was convinced that the TV show was too good to pass up, I decided—and my circle of trust agreed—I'd have to say no. In hindsight, it was the right decision.

I've made countless phone calls to my circle of trust. I know I'm wiser because of these amazing people. Like Proverbs 13:20 says,

"Walk with the wise and become wise; associate with fools and get in trouble" (NLT).

Do you have people in your life who will love you enough to tell you the truth, not just what you want to hear? Do you have people in your life who will challenge you to do the right thing, not influence you to do something you might regret? It doesn't have to be a big group of people. It works if you have just two or three friends you can trust, count on to pray for you, and encourage you in life and in your faith.

I remember when I first signed on with the Denver Broncos. Life was busy. I had just started my career in the NFL. I was living in a new city. I was with a new team. I was training nonstop. Because of my hectic schedule, I couldn't go to church every week. But I needed spiritual support. My friend Erik would call me every single day, no matter what city I was in or the time-zone difference. We would pray and have devotions. We did this even if we were sick, tired, frustrated, or didn't feel like it. I needed the consistency. And I appreciated his willingness to invest in me spiritually.

THE BEST KIND OF FRIEND

Having friends you can rely on is great. But consider this: What would your life look like if Jesus was your best friend? Does that sound weird or cool? One of my heroes in the Bible, a missionary named Paul who wrote most of the New Testament letters, gives a pretty good picture.

Before he became a Christian, Paul was part of a strict religious group that hated, even persecuted, Christians. After he met Jesus, he became a missionary, spreading the Good News throughout Asia Minor, Greece, and Rome. But Paul paid a price for his conversion. He was beaten. He was stoned. He was put in prison five times. Eventually, he was killed for his faith.

Paul was in prison when he wrote his letter to the Philippians. One of my favorite Bible verses is in this book: "I can do all things through Him who strengthens me" (4:13).

One of my pastors believes this prison held the storage system for all of Rome's sewage. Think of it as a holding tank for a giant toilet that served thousands upon thousands of people. Disgusting and smelly to say the least. Well, there Paul was, in chains, in what this pastor believes may have been a cell flooded with human waste up to his hips. I don't know about you, but if I were Paul, I probably would have been pretty upset about it.

But Paul wasn't. He wasn't bitter. He wasn't angry. In fact, he wrote verses about being able to do all things through Christ. And he wrote about joy, telling others how important it was to rejoice (see Philippians 4:4). Was he nuts? Out of his mind? A fool? No. He had a relationship with Jesus Christ. And he knew that since Jesus was his best friend, he could handle anything. He had a reason to rejoice. He had a reason to be confident. He had a reason to live.

So why would you want Jesus as your best friend? Simple. Because He died for you. Because He loves you. Because He has an awesome plan for your life. Because He will never leave you. Because when a friend, a sibling, or a teammate walks away, Jesus will be right by your side. He will be there for you through thick and thin. You might get discouraged because you didn't make the cut. Or a friend betrayed you. Or you're being pressured to drink or do drugs. Or someone made fun of you because of your outfit or because you go to church. But just remember, Jesus has your back.

Just remember, Jesus has your back.

When we enjoy healthy friendships, when we have a relationship with our ultimate friend, Jesus, and when we look out for others instead of ourselves, we will begin to live at our best. This will help us grow into who God created us to be. This will help us live in our uniqueness, be better than average, more than ordinary, far above "normal."

7

WHO SAID NORMAL IS THE GOAL?

If you are always trying to be normal, you will never know how amazing you can be.

—MAYA ANGELOU

R obyn was born on February 21, 2000, ten weeks early. Weighing only two pounds ten ounces, she could practically fit inside her parents' hands. Robyn was born so small and was so weak, doctors told her parents she was probably not going to live.

Robyn proved them wrong.

Though she survived and was able to leave the hospital after a month, Robyn was diagnosed with cerebral palsy (CP), a condition that affects the brain and movement. There are different degrees of CP, depending on the part of the brain and how bad the damage. But one-third of the people who have it can't walk, one-fourth have trouble talking, and three-fourths are in constant pain.[1]

When she was three, Robyn learned to walk with the help of a walker and knee braces. Tough and determined, she walked everywhere. She even learned how to ride a bike, one with three wheels because she couldn't balance. Though she doesn't remember falling much when she was younger, Robyn remembers how scary it was when she did. It wasn't that she would get badly hurt. It was that she wasn't able to get back up by herself. She would lie on the ground helpless until someone came and picked her up.

Robyn has endured countless shots and surgeries, weekly physical therapy, and constant pain. This had always been her life. She never thought of herself as different until she was in seventh grade and a classmate made fun of the way she walked. "For the first time, I realized that a walker wasn't normal," Robyn says. "I no longer saw it as something that gave me . . . freedom, but a magnet that attracted stares from strangers. Some days, all I could focus on was the walker. And when I looked in the mirror, I didn't see a teenage girl, I saw what I was convinced everyone else saw: a disability."

Robyn was fifteen when I met her briefly at our Celebrity Golf Classic, an annual event put on by the Tim Tebow Foundation. It's a weekend of fun for the kids that we love and support and also for our top donors and supporters of the foundation. Toward the end of the day, I walked over to the autograph area to sign books, footballs, and other items. The place was a madhouse. Many people who crowded the line looked impatient. Some of them even started pushing and shoving trying to get ahead. When I tried to see how far back the line ran, I caught sight of a blond-haired young lady. She was leaning on a walker. Even through the crowd I could see metal braces that covered her legs. But what I noticed most was how peaceful and content she seemed. It looked like she didn't even notice the people around her who were trying to push their way toward the front of the line. I couldn't believe some of them were practically knocking her over so they could fling books and footballs at me to sign. I mean, this was an event to honor kids who had special needs and disabilities!

It reminded me how we often miss what's right in front of us. I speak at a lot of events, to crowds in the hundreds and thousands. I realize that I don't see every single person who attends. But for some reason that day, I noticed this young lady. Just like I noticed Sherwin and his friends. I stopped signing photographs and made my way toward her. As I got close, her eyes lit up. So did mine.

"Hi, I'm Timmy," I said. "I'm so glad you're here!"

"I'm Robyn, with a *y*," she replied, cheerfully.

For just a few minutes, Robyn shared her story with me. I wished we had more time to talk, but I asked if I could stay in touch. A few months later, we granted her a W15H, one of my favorites. I celebrated her and her family in Atlanta with a special dinner, a spa day, and a VIP tour of the College Football Hall of Fame that focused on her love of the Florida Gators! Robyn and I spent hours talking. She told me that the past few months had been tough. The constant

> It reminded me how we often miss what's right in front of us.

stares at her walker reminded her in a painful way that she wasn't normal. Whether people said it to her face or looked at her weird, this made Robyn feel she wasn't special. That she didn't fit in. And it broke my heart.

I tried my best to encourage her. "Robyn, normal is average.

Being different is what makes you special and can give you the courage to treat others special," I said, as her eyes filled with tears. "God loves you, and you don't have to worry about anything else."

One year later, Robyn surprised me at the next Celebrity Golf Classic. She shared in front of a huge crowd a letter she wrote to me. I love what she said that night. "I used to think that my CP made me different in the worst way, but I have come to realize that my differences don't make me strange. They make me beautiful. Today, instead of seeing my walker as a problem, I see it as a platform . . . to influence lives. It's a way for me to inspire others."

Robyn still uses a walker and knee braces to get around. And though some people still stare at her, she is not bothered by being different. Robyn is not defined by what other people think. Or by society's definition of "normal." Or by those who say she is not special because she has CP. In fact, Robyn appreciates *not* being just like everybody else.

What's Normal, Anyway?

Fitting in, especially when you're younger, seems pretty important. And to do this usually means dressing like everyone else, listening to the same music as everyone else, hanging out where everyone else hangs out. You might know exactly what I'm talking about.

But I'm curious. What's normal, anyway? The dictionary defines it as "conforming to the standard or the common type; usual; regular." In other words, normal is being just like everyone else. Normal is safe. It doesn't require much work or effort. But keep in mind, normal always leads to being ordinary, so-so.

When we strive to be just like everyone else, we never have a chance to be special. When you start to accept and even celebrate how different God made you, you can begin to do extraordinary things. You can begin to see yourself through His eyes. You can begin to live in the unique way He created you. You can be motivated to go against the grain. What does that mean? When everyone around you is picking on someone, stand up for that person. When everyone around you is talking trash, say kind things instead.

Going against the norm can also mean having a different outlook on life than others do. When everyone around you is complaining there's too much homework, focus on how lucky you are to actually get an education. After all, millions of kids around the world don't even have a classroom to go to. And instead of trying to keep up with the latest trends, you can be grateful for what you have right now.

You matter too much to God to be just like everyone else.

CELEBRATE UNIQUE

I'm so thankful I am dyslexic. Yes, you read that right. I'm grateful for this learning disability. Now, I didn't always feel this way. When I was seven years old, I struggled to read. It was hard. My parents figured out I was dyslexic, which simply means I process things differently. I'm a tactile learner and have better success grasping concepts and ideas hands-on versus reading about them.

When I was twelve or thirteen years old, this learning challenge seemed the worst thing in the world. *Why can't I just pick up a book and read it like everyone else? Why does it have to take me hours and hours?* Spelling, memorizing, taking timed tests with essays—these things were nightmares. Going into high school, I wondered if I'd pass algebra, and later, if I'd make it through college. If you told me when I was young that I'd not only graduate from college but also maintain a 3.7 GPA, I'd have laughed in your face. I am so grateful for Susan Vanderlinde, my tutor growing up, whose knowledge and compassion made the learning process so much easier. She was a blessing!

Having a learning disability or any other type of disability doesn't mean you're dumb. Both Albert Einstein, the father of the atomic age, and Thomas Edison, one of the greatest inventors in history, were dyslexic. Now, I'm not comparing myself to these geniuses. They happen to be great examples of what's possible when you understand and make the most of the way you were created to learn.

I'm excited to be able to encourage kids and even adults who struggle with dyslexia. I know God is using that challenge as part of my platform. That's what He does. He takes something we see as a disability or a flaw, and He gives us opportunities to help people who struggle in those same areas. This is what Robyn has learned. She doesn't look at cerebral palsy as a disadvantage. She sees it as a platform she can use to help others.

I have never woken up once in my life saying I wanted to be normal, average. I never wanted to be like anyone else. I always wanted to be special. My parents helped me develop this mind-set. They repeatedly told me and my siblings,

"God has a special plan for you."

"You are not like everyone else."

"You are unique."

This helped to lay a solid foundation of identity in my life. Now, I understand not everyone has parents who are super encouraging. But just because our families may not have told us how special we are doesn't mean we're not. We just might have to work harder to believe it.

Let's get back to our identity in God. He created each of us in a unique way for a reason. We are each different in how we look, how we think, how we learn. We also have different backgrounds and experiences. If you were born with a disability, if you don't think you're as smart or as cool as your older brother or sister, if you struggle physically, you might have said something like,

> I like to think of parts of the Bible as a collection of love letters He wrote for His children.

"God must have made a mistake."

"I don't like being me."

"I wish I were someone else."

If so, stop right there. God would disagree.

I like to think of parts of the Bible as a collection of love letters He wrote for His children. One of them powerfully tells us how wonderful we are, how special He purposely made us. I'd like you to read these words out loud to God as if you wrote them.

You made all the delicate, inner parts of my body
    and knit me together in my mother's womb.
Thank you for making me so wonderfully complex!
    Your workmanship is marvelous—how well
        I know it.
You watched me as I was being formed in utter seclusion,
    as I was woven together in the dark of the womb.
You saw me before I was born.
    Every day of my life was recorded in your book.
Every moment was laid out
    before a single day had passed.

How precious are your thoughts about me, O God.
    They cannot be numbered!
I can't even count them;
    they outnumber the grains of sand!
        (Psalm 139:13–18, NLT)

If you're having a hard time fitting in, if you feel you aren't pretty enough, strong enough, big enough, fast enough, or smart enough, know that God created you perfect. You are not an accident. You are not a mistake. You are wonderfully made.

Don't get beaten down when others point out how different you are, look, or act. They don't know God's plan for your life. They don't know how God can use what they may see as a weakness. When you begin to accept how God purposely created you, you can begin to appreciate your uniqueness. And you can allow Him to use you to help others.

God gave you whatever challenges you have for a reason. If you're feeling discouraged, know that He has your best interest at heart. Remember, His love is perfect. And He loves you perfectly. We may see ourselves as unworthy, unusable, flawed, or broken, but God looks at us as shining stars. He thinks about us all the time. His thoughts for us are precious. Know that what you might consider a flaw—whether a scar, an illness, or a learning disability—is actually something beautiful and intentional to fulfill God's purpose for you.

WHAT YOU HAVE TO OFFER

When I talk about how special each one of us is, I'm not talking about the way society sees us. We are not special just because we got on the honor roll again this semester. Or got the lead part in the play. Or helped win the state championship for our team. I'm talking about the uniqueness God created us with—the gifts, talents, and abilities that make up who we are.

Think about what you're good at, the one-of-a-kind traits that are hardwired in you. Think about what you love to do. Maybe you are a talented musician or athlete. You may be a natural leader, skilled at building things, or a gifted artist. You may be great at performing or brilliant in science. You might be compassionate or have a servant's heart. Instead of wanting to be like someone else, make the most of your talents. The Bible teaches that "God has given each of you a gift from his great variety of spiritual gifts. Use them well to serve one another."[2]

Use what He has given you. Practice your skills. Work on them. Don't let them waste away. Whether it's singing, speaking, serving, or working with numbers, use your gifts to make a positive impact on this world.

My friend Judah says, "The Christian faith is about living life with an open hand, using the gifts and blessings in our lives for others. Like a conveyor belt, we simply get to touch the blessings and the gifts as they keep moving out toward others. We are blessed to be a blessing. When we stop the flow, the blessings stop." Don't hold on to your gifts. Share them. Use them to serve. Use them to make a difference.

Don't strive to be like someone else. Be who God created you to be. Be you.

One more thing. Let God be God. Allow Him to use what you bring to Him, however He chooses. There's nothing wrong with dreaming big. I do this all the time! But how God ultimately unfolds the plan of your life through these gifts is up to Him. You might love basketball and play the game well, but you might not be the next LeBron James.

Work on your gifts and talents in a way that challenges you. Don't compare your skill level to anyone else. It's okay to want to be the best, but it's more important to want to be *your* best.

I promise you this: God will use your gifts, talents, and abilities in His way and for His plan. It might be to change the life of one person or one million. Rather than focus on trying to figure out or influence how He will make it happen, focus on Him.

THE PROBLEM OF PRIDE

While some people may struggle with not knowing what they have to offer, others know exactly what that is. And sometimes, they forget that "every good thing given and every perfect gift is from above, coming down from the Father" (James 1:17).

I'll always remember one particular Sunday at church with my family. I was in the third grade. Even then I was a competitive beast. While God had blessed me with athletic skill, as a child I wasn't mature enough to realize that my talent came from God. Oh sure, I was taught the Bible and the principles of Jesus, and I knew the truth in my head. The problem had to do with my heart. At the time, my passion for scoring touchdowns, hitting home runs, and winning games was all I thought about.

After the church service, my parents stopped to talk to some friends. This couple had four kids, similar in ages to my siblings. This family didn't have a child my age, so I stood by while my two sisters chatted it up with two other siblings. Hoping to get in with the older kids, I tried to make my way into their conversation. For the life of me I can't remember exactly what I said, but I know for a fact that it was stupid and arrogant. I blurted out something along the lines of "I'm better in baseball than everyone in my grade!" Then I turned to one of the guys my sisters were talking to and said, "I'm sure I can beat you, too!" Oh, and I said this in my loudest, most confident voice.

I told you, not too smart.

As soon as that last word flew out of my mouth, my two sisters looked at me, horrified. My heart sank. I knew I had disappointed them deeply. My sisters were two people I looked up to so much. Katie was always so much fun and awesome to hang with, and Christy was always full of wisdom and a great role model. These were two of the coolest people on the planet. I was so embarrassed.

I remembered back to being four or five, when after winning a handful of T-ball games, I blabbed to everyone who would listen about my wins. Mom and Dad used this teachable moment to create a new house rule. Before each game, I had to memorize a Bible verse about humility. Every. Single. Game. I don't know why I said what I said that Sunday, but it seems in that moment I forgot about everything my parents had taught me about being humble (see Proverbs 16:18; Proverbs 29:23; Philippians 2:3).

I can clearly picture the walk from the church to our car, which was probably a good quarter of a mile. I lagged behind, feeling ashamed. All I had wanted to do was to look cool in front of my two big sisters, you know, fit in with the older kids. And I thought I could impress them by saying something impressive about myself. As I trudged toward the car, afraid that my

You can be confident without boasting.

foolish words would make them never want to talk to me again, I promised myself never to say something stupid like that again.

Look, you can be confident without boasting. When we show off the talents, gifts, and abilities God has given us, it shreds our true identity. We forget whose we are. We forget where our blessings come from. We take credit for what God did in us. The Bible challenges, "For who regards you as superior? What do you have that you did not receive? And if you did receive it, why do you boast as if you had not received it?"[3]

When we perform, whether playing sports or music, it's easy to want to point to ourselves and show the world how awesome we performed. After all, wins and awards require work. And when we put in the work, there is a tendency to want to show off.

While it's important to be self-confident, we need balance. We must be proud of our accomplishments without letting them define us. Awards don't last. You may have been named Most Likely to Succeed in school, but the next year, nobody cares. There is always going to be another winner after you. This is why we need to live knowing whose we are. When we fix our identity in the One who created us, we can keep pride at bay. And we can give whatever praise may come our way to the One worthy of it.

BEING MORE THAN AVERAGE
REQUIRES COURAGE

True story: A man I'll call John was walking to the local burger joint to grab a bite to eat. Just as he stepped into the parking lot, a young man with special needs, a visible scar on his neck, and facial deformities came up to him. As he had recently injured his foot, John was wearing a walking boot. The young man asked, "What happened to your foot?"

"I hurt it working out," John replied. He felt uncomfortable as he wondered why a stranger would strike up a random conversation in a parking lot.

"Can I pray for you?" the young man asked.

John's first thought was, *What a weirdo!* But a split second later, he was quick to realize how courageous the young man was to ask a stranger if he could pray for him. And John felt humbled, admiring the guy for daring to do something different.

"Sure," John responded. "I would appreciate it." He assumed the young man would walk away and pray for him in private, but that's not what happened. In John's own words, "What made this guy even more courageous was that he got down on his knee, placed a hand on my boot, and prayed right there. It made me realize that when you're doing things for the greater good there is no need to be embarrassed or ashamed or wonder how people are going to perceive you because the only opinion that matters comes from above."

When is the last time you did something different? Something beyond your comfort zone? When you stay put in your comfort zone, you don't grow. You don't stretch. You're not challenged. You stay the same.

I remember being in eighth grade and being a part of a missions outreach. My youth group visited an arcade that was packed with thirty or so young people playing Skee-Ball, pinball, and air hockey. One of the leaders asked us kids, "Who wants to get up and preach?"

All eyes fell to the floor and stayed there. I volunteered. I didn't really want to, but no one else raised a hand. At the same time I said yes, my mind started racing. *What if I forget what I'm supposed to say? What if my words come out wrong? What if no one listens? What if they laugh at me?* When it was time to talk, as afraid as I was, I spoke from the heart. I may not have been smooth with my words or shared the gospel with perfection, but I was sincere. And I was blown away when, by the grace of God, a handful of kids responded positively to the message of Jesus.

It's okay to feel afraid while taking the first step. I love the title of the book *Feel the Fear . . . and Do It Anyway!* Doing something against the flow of the crowd will probably feel uncomfortable and scary. Do it anyway.

Be who God created you to be.

Be bold. Brave. Courageous.

8

STAND UP

**If you don't stand for something,
you'll fall for anything.**

—UNKNOWN

About a thousand high-school kids flocked to the camp-grounds. I'd never seen so many teenagers in one place in my life. It was my first time being at a Christian camp that hosted multiple churches. It was also my first time being around so many high schoolers in one place. A few weeks shy of fifteen, I wasn't intimidated by the crowd. I felt confident. I was going to dominate. I was going to get to know people. I was going to talk to a bunch of girls. And I was going to crush every one of the week's many sports competitions.

I was excited to be at that camp for a few reasons—not just for the five hundred or so girls that I could potentially meet. My broth-ers, both great athletes, were there, too. Peter, who was a senior in high school at the time, was one of the older kids. And Robby was there as one of three hundred counselors. It was like the dream team. My brothers and I were prepared to have the time of our lives.

We were particularly stoked for the basketball tournament, the main attraction of all the events. While I was bummed to not be on

Robby's team, Peter and I were on the same team, which had some pretty decent athletes. We weren't great, but we were tough. Whoever we played was guaranteed to have a tough time beating us.

The basketball tournament started out with forty or so teams. And as the days passed, the bracket got smaller and smaller. Peter and I played our hearts out. No guts, no glory. Our team killed it, clinching our spot in the final four. Robby's team also made it to the semifinals. If they won their game and we won ours, we would play each other in the championship round.

The entire camp gathered outside under the lights to watch Robby's team play. All eyes were glued to the action. Except for Robby, every player on his team was a camper, a high-school student. The opposing team was made up of camp counselors, who were college kids.

It was a dirty game from the start. I stood near the sidelines watching the drama unfold. The opposing team took cheap shots, and they bodychecked my brother and his teammates. My blood boiled. I stormed over and stood just under the basket, yelling out in protest. By now, the crowds on either side of me were on their feet cheering or jeering, depending on which team they were rooting for.

The score bounced back and forth for a while, not more than four points different. For sure, Robby dominated the game. But the opposing team pushed and fouled him constantly along the way. Though my brother was by far the best player in that game, the other guys had the better team. And though he was a force to be reckoned with, Robby and his teammates lost.

Then it was our turn to play. Peter and I took charge of the court, leading our teammates to victory and into the finals. We had barely fifteen minutes before it was time to face the punk team that had beaten Robby's. I didn't care. I felt I could run for days. So could Peter. Together, we were unstoppable.

After the tipoff, I ran up and down that court, slamming basket after basket. I may have been just a freshman in high school, but I blasted those college guys. Sure, I wanted to win, but this game was more than that. It was personal. They had played dirty and beaten my brother.

As I shot a couple of different lay-ups, one of the opposing players shoved me from behind. It was an obvious foul, but no one called it. I didn't get physical in response, but I warned this camp counselor to chill out. He didn't listen.

Both teams dueled it out in an epic back-and-forth battle. The other team kept getting more and more physical with Peter and me especially. I tried to dodge an elbow here, a shoulder there while scoring point after point. As the opposing players busted out with loudmouth trash talk, Robby stood on the sidelines. Veins popping out of his neck, he called them out for their cheap shots. I scanned the court for a ref, waiting to hear a whistle. Nothing.

Bam! Someone tried to slam me off my feet from behind. I turned to the player and repeated the warning to chill out. He gave me what he thought was a threatening stone-cold look. With sweat flying off my face, I said to this college dude, "Just trust me. You don't want to do that." I meant it. Football season was only a few weeks away, and I didn't want to get hurt. Peter was also getting ready to play his senior year; he didn't want to get hurt either.

Fourth quarter. Peter stole the ball and took off down the court at full speed. As he ran, an opposing player tackled him from behind. My brother fell to the ground, cutting up his knees and elbows on the rough asphalt. While the crowd went bananas, the guy who pushed Peter stood over him, talking smack. I didn't know what he was going to do next, so I rushed to my brother's defense. I put a shoulder to the player who knocked Peter down. And then, chaos.

Let's just say for a few minutes my brothers and I and players from both teams started shoving and pushing each other. Here's the thing. Peter, Robby, and I had no intention of starting a fight. All we wanted to do was protect one another. I, for one, was making a statement: don't ever touch my brother like that again.

Finally, everyone calmed down enough to finish the quarter. But not before I got kicked out of the game. And while just before the brawl our team was up 68–62, with Peter hurting and me on the bench, we lost.

Okay, I admit: I didn't do a great job that day of showing Jesus. And I certainly am not condoning fights on the court or on the field. While my character may have been questionable in throwing a shoulder, I was focused on one thing—standing up for my brother. That's all I could think about.

In hindsight, yeah, I probably shouldn't have checked that one player and instead just helped Peter up. While I might not have done what mattered most, I showed my brother that he mattered. I chose to take a stand for him. I chose to defend him and fight for him. I chose to have his back. I'm not saying the way I showed Peter he mattered was the right way, but my heart was in the right place.

I'm not fifteen anymore, and over the years I've worked to tame that young arrogance. And though I have a fiercely competitive nature—that'll never change—I strive to keep growing in maturity and stand for things that really matter in the big picture. Like Sherwin and kids like him who have disabilities or illnesses. And obviously, my faith.

> **If you don't stand for something, you'll fall for anything.**

I'm a big believer in the statement "If you don't stand for something, you'll fall for anything." What does it mean to take a stand? It's pretty simple. It's standing up for something or someone you believe in. Every single one of us has the power to do that.

Standing up is a way of life. Pay attention to opportunities where you can make a positive difference. Find a need and fill it. You can do this in big ways and small ways. Volunteer for a local food pantry. Use your allowance to donate to a worthy cause. Pray for someone. Shovel snow or mow the lawn for an elderly neighbor. Offer to tutor a student who is struggling in math. Make sandwiches for the homeless. Sit next to someone at lunch who is sitting alone.

Another way to figure out what it means for you to take a stand is to ask yourself, *What am I known for?* Are you known for playing video games all day? Bingeing on Netflix? Or are you known for loving people? Being generous? Being a faithful friend? Being kind to strangers?

In the last chapter, we talked about how we don't need to be "normal," just like everyone else. Taking a stand for something is a great way to live an extraordinary life.

KEEP IT SIMPLE

The stand you take may not be the biggest deal to the entire world, but it can be a big deal for one person. For instance, you may not be able to feed all of Africa, but you can feed one person. Taking a stand for one person can make more of a difference than you may realize.

Recently, someone shared with me something he did in middle school that made a big difference. At the time, however, he didn't think it was a big deal. Here's what happened. One of his classmates was a loner who had autism. Every single day, a group of bullies would pick on this kid. They'd push him around and kick over the wheeled backpack he pulled along. The young man who told me this story had watched this scene play out day after day after day. And one day, seeing this kid picked on for no reason, he got fed up. He went up to the leader of the pack and, in a calm way, asked him a question: "Why are you doing this?"

Without even knowing it, this young man put the bully on the spot. While the bully didn't say anything in response, neither he nor anyone else ever bothered that kid again. Later, the classmate who was picked on thanked the young man. "For what?" he replied. "I didn't even do anything." Well, he may not have slapped the bully upside the head. Or yelled in his face. Or threatened him. But he stepped up and asked a question, a challenging one. And this one simple act made all the difference in the world to the kid who was being picked on.

> **Right that wrong. Be part of the solution. This is what it means to take a stand.**

I've been pretty vocal about my beliefs and have taken stands on many things—even a knee now and then. You may wonder what you can possibly take a stand for. It's simple, really. Have you ever seen someone hurting? Have you ever seen something wrong? Have you ever been faced with a problem you could fix? Then help that person. Right that wrong. Be part of the solution. This is what it means to take a stand.

I'll never forget one of the first times I drove into New York City after signing on with the Jets. I was stopped at a red light. Although I was six or seven cars from the intersection, I noticed an older man wearing dark glasses and carrying a white support cane, the kind used by people who are blind. Surrounding him was classic New York traffic—a sea of beeping taxis, the masses rushing across busy city streets.

Moving maybe a car length or two with each changing light, I watched this man attempt to cross the street. Three times he tried to make his way a few steps into the flow of the foot traffic, tapping his cane along the way, but then he'd stop partway in and take a few steps back toward the curb. He seemed overwhelmed. And not one person helped this guy cross the street.

I wanted to get out of the car and help him but was strongly advised not to. You know, that whole media-attention thing. Looking back, I regret not doing the right thing. Even though I was several lanes over from where this man was, I should have listened to my gut and made the effort instead of listening to those who told me not to.

Sitting in the car that day, I was mad. I remember thinking, *What's the matter with people?* This was a golden opportunity for people to get off their phones, stop checking their Likes on Facebook or Instagram, stop thinking about only themselves, and take a stand. Yes, even just by something as simple as helping someone cross the street. Something that takes only a few minutes to do. Something that doesn't require a talent, a skill, or much time.

Taking a stand requires willingness. Find a need and fill it. Ask God to put something or someone on your heart. Do something different. He will use whatever you can offer for a greater purpose.

WHAT GOD CAN DO

I was in college, getting ready to face Miami, when for the first time I wanted to do something different with my eye black. I remember being in the training room, getting ready to pick up my eye-black strips, when I started wondering what I could write that would inspire someone else.

Philippians 4:13 immediately came to mind: "I can do all things through Him who strengthens me." It's a great verse for football and a great verse for life and faith. While this has long been one of my favorites—and a verse that's often quoted—it's important to understand the context to fully understand the meaning.

In the text leading up to verse 13, Paul, the man who wrote the book of Philippians, said, "I know what it is to be in need, and I know what it is to have plenty. I have learned the secret of being content in any and every situation, whether well fed or hungry, whether living in plenty or in want" (Philippians 4:12, NIV). These verses explain that Paul was talking about being content when he followed with "I can do all things." He was saying, "I can handle the good. I can handle the bad. I can handle whatever the world throws at me because my relationship with Jesus is rock solid. He'll see me through the storms." Paul knew not just how to survive but how to crush it in both good times and bad.

That game, a few people noticed the verse. I kept putting it on my eye black every week for the rest of the regular season. I remember running out of the tunnel right before we Gators faced Alabama in the 2008 SEC Championship. In my heart I felt God nudging me to change the verse. But I wasn't sure to which one. After a few days, the one that kept coming to mind was John 3:16, the core of God's heart for us. "For God so loved the world, that He gave His only begotten Son, that whoever believes in Him shall not perish, but have eternal life."

When I told my parents about it, Mom was thrilled. Dad, however, was hesitant. "You know how Coach likes his routine, Timmy. Don't mess with that," he warned. Well, Coach Meyer was a pretty superstitious guy. If we won with our socks pulled up, we'd have to keep them up for the next game. But Coach ultimately gave me his blessing.

On January 8, 2009, during the National Championship game, I wore "John 3:16" on my eye black. After we defeated Oklahoma, Coach, my parents, and I ate dinner together at a restaurant in Gainesville. As we chowed down, his phone rang. Coach had a short conversation with the person calling.

"Yep." Pause.

"Uh-huh." Pause.

"Oh." Pause.

"Okay, then." Pause.

"Goodbye, now."

"Well," Coach said as he turned to us with a smile, "I was just told that ninety-four million people Googled 'John 3:16' during the game!"

Wow! Talk about humbling. God is so big that He used something so small, a tiny biblical reference painted under my eyes, to influence people to search His Word.

I wore different verses my senior year. Most of the verses I chose made it to the top spot on Google Trends, which told me that many people wanted to know what these verses said. I felt honored when fans started a group on Facebook that rallied the Gator Nation to wear eye blacks during my last home game in the Swamp—many of them with their favorite Bible verse on it.

Exactly three years after wearing "John 3:16" for the first time, I was playing for the Broncos. NFL rules kept me from wearing personalized messages on my eye blacks. But still, without any help from me, the John 3:16 theme continued. In one of the most memorable games in my career, we beat the heavily favored Steelers 29–23.

Our team's publicity guy flagged me down just before my post-game press conference. "Hey, Timmy," Patrick blurted out, "do you have any idea what happened?"

I started to make a joke but stopped when I noticed how serious he looked. Like he was just about to tell me something really important.

"Do you know that it was exactly three years since you wore 'John 3:16'? And during this game, you threw for 316 yards. Your yards per completion were 31.6. The time of possession was 31:06. The ratings for the night were 31.6 million. And during the game ninety million people Googled 'John 3:16'!"

Wow! To think that all those years ago, all I had wanted was just to do something different with eye black. I felt so small in that moment. I didn't know it was exactly three years later. And I didn't know what God was doing or that He was even doing anything at all. I was focused on doing what I needed to do to win a playoff game.

That day I was reminded that God is a big God. And He is always at work—with or without me. Just goes to show you that we never know what God can do with the small choices we make, with the stands we take, or with something positive we do even when we don't realize it.

It's amazing what God can do when you are willing to do something different. Some people may not understand what you're doing. Some may think you're crazy for doing it. But know that God can take that willingness and do amazing things through it, even when you don't have a clue. Because that's how big He is.

Stay True to Who You Are

In chapter 3 I talked about my first game starting for the Denver Broncos. Though the Miami Dolphins had crushed us for most of the game, in the fourth quarter, on the verge of getting shut out for the first time since 1992, we turned it around. I helped lead our team to a double-digit comeback to win in overtime.

This was the kind of comeback moment I dreamed about as a little boy. So when winning seemed impossible and our team rallied and flipped our losing streak on its back, I was beside myself. I'll never forget what happened immediately after Matt Prater nailed the game-winning fifty-two-yard field goal. It was like the field blew up. Every Broncos teammate, coach, and staff member rushed onto the grass while the fans in the stadium went wild. As I ran a few steps onto the field, adrenaline pounding, I got down on one knee, my elbow resting on the other, fist to my forehead, head bowed. Yep, I "Tebowed."

This wasn't a celebration stance or even a public stance for my faith. It was a reminder of who was in charge. I had to humble myself in the middle of this victory, remembering and thanking God for everything He'd done for me. The win wasn't about me. Taking a knee and saying a prayer of thanks was a way of keeping my heart in the right place. It was about submitting to God. And it was also something I'd always done with intention.

If you look at some of my pre-NFL games, I took a knee often. I did it after the Gators lost to Alabama in the 2009 SEC Championship. I did it before games in high school. And most times I did it on the sidelines, away from the frenzy. Whether in victory or loss, Tebowing, in my mind, turned the attention away from me and pointed toward God. I've always wanted to remind myself on purpose that no matter the huge win or the crushing loss, God is bigger than those things. And bigger than me.

I can't tell you how many people have come up to me and said, "Hey, you're that guy who takes a knee after touchdowns." I just smile and nod. Truth is, I've never done that as a touchdown celebration. But the day we beat Miami in overtime and I took a knee as our team and fans celebrated, a cameraman focused in on me. Funny, at the same time, a Denver native named Jared Kleinstein and a group of his friends who had watched the game in New York City took a picture of themselves Tebowing. He uploaded the photo to his Facebook account, and it started trending. In the next few days, Jared created the *Tebowing* Tumblr blog and purchased the Tebowing domain name for ten dollars.

Suddenly, Tebowing became the new thing. Everyone was doing it—celebrities at award shows, high-school students during athletic events, players during NBA games, even presidential candidates. It even became an official word in the English language, defined as "the act of 'taking a knee' in prayerful reflection in the midst of an athletic activity."[1] Another definition I've read is "to get down on a knee and start praying, even if everyone else around you is doing something completely different."[2]

> **Taking a stand doesn't always mean doing something radical.**

Now, I'm not the first athlete to take a knee and pray or thank God. And it's not like I set out that day purposely to do something that would attract attention. It's funny, the next week when we faced the Detroit Lions, linebacker Stephen Tulloch Tebowed on top of me after he sacked me in the second quarter.

Taking a stand doesn't always mean doing something radical. Sometimes God will use something you've always done in a way that's bigger than you can imagine. Sometimes He'll use something He puts on your heart. He might even use your desire to do the right thing for a greater purpose.

Want to be a stand-taker? Stay true to your faith. Be kind. Be compassionate. Help someone who needs it. Turn off that video game and ask your little brother or sister how they're doing. Do the right thing. Don't watch what everybody else is watching or do what everyone else is doing if you know it's wrong. Be brave. Stand up for what you believe in.

Standing up for something you believe in is not always easy. You may get some flak. You may get criticized. Winston Churchill said, "You have enemies? Good. That means you've stood up for something, sometime in your life."[3] While *enemies* might be a strong word, don't get sidetracked by those who don't believe in you or by those who don't understand what you are doing. Whenever you dare to do something different, there's going to be someone who doesn't get it and might even make a big stink about it.

And sometimes in the process of standing up for something, you may make a mistake or fail in some way, which will likely attract more critics. News flash: I'm nowhere near perfect. I try to be a good role model. I try to do and think the right things. But I'm human. I mess up. I have failed and let people down. I certainly don't belong on a pedestal. Jesus is the only One who belongs on a pedestal. The rest of us are sinners. This is why we need Jesus. Apart from God's grace, not one of us is whole or complete or righteous.

So today, think about what you can do to make life a little bit better, maybe even a little bit easier for someone else. Are you willing to gather up some canned foods and donate them to a local soup kitchen? Or do the right thing even though no one else is doing it? Or pray for someone in public? Or write a thank-you note to a veteran or police officer? Or share your faith? Or stand up for people who can't stand up for themselves? Or say no when everyone else is saying yes? Or say yes when everyone else is saying no?

What stand are you willing to take?

FAMILY

GATOR DAYS

JOHN 3:16

MY ONLY PERSONAL FOUL

FIGHTING FOR EVERY YARD

FIRED UP

SPECIAL MOMENT

TIED IT UP, HEADED TO OVERTIME

DAY ONE AS A BRONCO

GIVING THANKS

SHARING GOD'S LOVE WITH SOME INMATES IN PRISON

SOME OF MY FILIPINO BROTHERS AND SISTERS

TEBOW CURE HOSPITAL

LOVE THIS CREW

MY BUDDY BOOMER

I'LL NEVER FORGET MY FRIEND
CHELSIE, A MIGHTY WARRIOR

LISTENING TO JAKE OWEN WITH
BLAINE, ANSLEY, AND KELLY AT
THE TTF GALA

ENJOYING TIME WITH ROBYN,
EVEN AT A GEORGIA BULLDOGS GAME

Photo by Allison Alexander Fowler

DATE NIGHT AT NIGHT TO SHINE,
CHARLOTTE, NC

Photo by Lauren Bowser

INTRODUCING GARY LEVOX
FROM RASCAL FLATTS AS HE
PREPARES TO TAKE THE STAGE
AT NIGHT TO SHINE

Photo by Sara Beth Turner

ONE OF OUR QUEENS FROM NIGHT TO SHINE, HAITI

9

THE POWER OF
DOING SOMETHING

**Action is the foundational
key to all success.**

—Pablo Picasso

've never heard God speak out loud. No booming voice. No lightning bolt from the sky. In my first book, *Through My Eyes,* I talked about how hard it was to decide between playing for the Florida Gators and the Alabama Crimson Tide. I had solid relationships with both head coaches. And I admired them equally. Both schools were competitive and top rated. I prayed and prayed. My family did the same.

When decision day came, I didn't have an answer. How do you choose between something great and something just as great? The clock was ticking. It was just minutes before ESPN started filming my college decision for the presentation of the Florida Dairy Farmers High School Player of the Year award, and I still didn't know what I was going to say. Finally, when the mics were on and the cameras started rolling, I announced, "I will be playing college football next year at the University of Florida."

Though I trust in God and aim to seek what He wants for my life, there are many times I get stuck not knowing what to do. Do I say yes to this event or that one? Do I accept this offer or that one? Do I support this hospital, that child, this charity, or that business idea? The list is long.

Does this make me a bad Christian? Of course not. It makes me human. This hearing-from-God stuff can be tricky. I definitely believe He speaks to people in different ways. The Bible is one way. God's Word tells us that "all Scripture is inspired by God and is useful to teach us what is true and to make us realize what is wrong in our lives."[1] I also believe we can hear God in our hearts through wise counsel, from those we trust. I can tell you that when I have to make a tough decision, I pray long and hard. I try to listen to what I feel God puts on my heart. I seek wise counsel. And I reflect on what's most important to me. And then I am forced to make a decision.

Though I've never heard God's actual voice, I have felt drawn to notice certain people. Like Sherwin and his friends, like Robyn. I believe God works in my life this way. While He didn't tell me out loud to find Sherwin or to stop what I was doing to talk to Robyn, I feel like He moved my heart to pay attention to them.

I know how hard it can be when we're not sure what God wants us to do. Sometimes, this not knowing can lead us to do nothing. Look, while there are times we need to wait on God before making a decision, there is rarely a time to do absolutely nothing.

You know what happens when we do nothing? Nothing.

I've talked about the importance of taking stands to make a difference. This requires action. There is always something to do.

Pay attention.

Look around.

Listen.

God just might be speaking.

JUST SAY YES

Since I was a freshman in college, I've visited about twelve American prisons, many of them multiple times. There I shared with inmates the love and hope of Jesus. I remember like it was yesterday my first time visiting a prison. As I stood in the yard surrounded by a high fence, I stared into the hardened faces of men doing time. Some had pretty scary-looking tattoos. I'll admit, I felt overwhelmed. It was one thing to talk to men behind bars. It's another thing to stand right beside them, giving them hugs and shaking their hands. That can be intimidating. I was also just a nineteen-year-old kid. And many of the men in the yard had years of life experience on me. My mind raced. *How am I going to do this? What am I going to say?*

I remembered a radio interview I had done recently. The host had asked if I would consider myself a success. I said yes, but not because of football. It was because I have a relationship with Jesus Christ. I told the men in that prison yard a slightly tweaked version of what I had told the radio host. I told them that I had a relationship with the God of the universe and that they could, too. I told them that although some people on the outside may have forgotten about them, there was one man who never would—Jesus. The moment I started sharing the message on my heart, I felt at peace. I closed my talk with an invitation. "If you want to trust Jesus," I said, "I'd love for you to stand up and stand right next to me." I'll never forget the big guy in the front row of the crowd, a hard-looking dude. I'd seen him before I started talking. Imagine my surprise when he stood up and made his way beside me. I can't even begin to tell you how grateful I was.

Fast-forward almost ten years. I was on my way to visit Florida State Prison with Jim Williams, a man who has been working in prison ministry for more than forty-two years. Erik and Robby came, too. We were eager to see what God had in store for us.

> We prayed under our breath while waiting for the warden.

The sky was overcast that day. It matched the color of the prison property. A steel sign welcomed us. It stretched from one side of the roadway to the other, blaring "Florida State Prison." Up ahead, grim-looking concrete buildings were surrounded by a high chain-link fence that was stacked with rows of razor-wire spirals. It looked creepy. Like something out of a scary movie. We walked into one of the buildings. Guards stood in the hallway. We prayed under our breath while waiting for the warden, a man I had met before. A strong Christian, he's tough but loves the inmates and treats them with decency. I like that.

The warden welcomed us, then gave us instructions: "Don't get too close. Remember, these men are dangerous. Make sure you stand about an arm's length away from the cell."

— 156 —

I break this rule all the time. Though I'm not technically allowed to shake an inmate's hand, I do it anyway. Call me an old-fashioned southern boy, but it's the right thing to do. And yeah, there have been times my friendliness was not appreciated.

The warden continued, "Also, don't get into small talk, like the weather. Some of these guys have been stuck inside four walls for a while. They don't know whether it's sunny or cloudy, and they don't need to be reminded of that."

Jim, Robby, Erik, and I then walked into another building. On our way to a particular cell block, we talked to other inmates. A few of them, familiar with college ball, started yelling my name and doing the Gator chomp. Another noticed and started talking smack in response.

After sharing a bit with these men, we continued our journey. The warden led us down one of many long and dark hallways we would walk through that day. After passing a few stony-faced guards, we reached our destination—death row. Prisoners in this section have committed serious crimes and have been sentenced to be put to death. They spend twenty-three hours of each day in these six-by-nine-foot cells.

The first inmate I spoke to recognized me right away. "Hey," he called out in a friendly tone. "Why aren't you playing for the Jaguars?"

As I'd always done, I ignored the warden's warning and stepped right up to the bars of the cell. We talked for a bit. He told me he had read the Bible a few times and found it boring. I told him that God loved him and had a plan for his life, even though it may not seem like it from behind bars. I shared with him the story of how Jesus was condemned to die alongside two other criminals. One of them decided to believe in Him. I shared how we've all sinned and fallen short and that it's never too late to change our eternal fate. He listened respectfully but wasn't interested.

The four of us offered words of hope to these men, one by one. We could feel God's presence, even in a place full of despair. It's why we felt so comfortable standing only an inch or two away from some of the most violent criminals in the country.

Before we left that part of the prison, we celebrated one inmate's decision to accept the gift of grace that Jesus gives to all who believe. We gave him a Bible, writing on the inside flap, "April 7, 2015. A new start." Robby grabbed the guy's hand through the steel bars and pulled him as close as he could in a hug and said, "Welcome to the family!"

When it was time to go, I felt drained. Sharing in this environment is a very emotional experience. It's filled with highs and lows. You talk to some guys who are excited to hear a message of hope and others who couldn't care less. The differences are extreme. And it can zap your energy level. Make you feel drained. As I walked back down a series of dark hallways, I caught a glimpse of light at the end of the corridor. There was something comforting about it. I was ready to go home.

But instead of turning left toward the light, the warden asked if we would spend some time with the prison nurses in the medical ward. They had been going through a tough time. We said yes, then made a right turn down another dark corridor. A half hour or more had passed after this pit stop when I noticed Erik looking around, curious. He pointed to a mystery hallway and asked the warden, "What's down there?"

I'm not proud to say this, but in that moment I didn't want to know. I just wanted to go home. I was running on empty.

But when the warden told us what was down that hallway, I felt God leading me to go there. Sometimes people lose hope. When that happens, they can be at risk for hurting themselves . . . or worse. And when prisoners get to that place, the prison staff needs to watch over them more closely. They do what needs to be done so the inmates stay safe. This cellblock is called suicide watch.

Feeling prompted to visit the men here who had threatened to harm themselves, I walked, not far, and stood in front of four side-by-side protective cells. Each cell had padded walls and a steel door with a small, cloudy plexiglass window and, underneath, a slot where meals were served. To ensure their safety, prisoners are forced to wear what look like straitjackets and restraints on their ankles.

I felt God leading me to go there.

I walked up to the first cell. The door and walls were so thick, I had to press my face right against the thick window and talk real loudly. The first guy I talked to said nothing. His eyes were blank. I took a few steps over to the next cell, introduced myself, and started sharing. Same response.

Before I got close to the third cell, the warden grabbed my arm and told me how the man in this cell had tried to harm himself a few days ago. This prisoner was in a real desperate situation.

I nodded, but I didn't know what to expect. As I grabbed a sip of water, the warden took a few steps ahead of me and pressed his face into the window of this third cell. "Hey, buddy. You have a special visitor you might want to come see."

I switched places with the warden and peered into the smudged window. The view was blurry, but I could see a man inside wearing a straitjacket. He started shuffling his way toward me. He pressed his face against the window and we locked eyes. He looked younger than me. Immediately, the man gasped in shock and exclaimed, "You're a Christian!" I hadn't seen this type of reaction from any of the other prisoners that day.

"Yes sir. I am. Do you know why we're here?"

"No."

"We're here to tell you that God loves you."

At some point Erik said, "I think we are here specifically to tell *you* that."

When the young man heard these words, he crumpled to the floor like a rag doll. Tears poured down his face. His shoulders shook in violent sobs.

I was speechless, watching a hardened criminal cry like a baby. It took a few minutes for him to pull himself together. Unable to use his arms, he struggled to stand up and awkwardly stumbled his way back to the window.

"Let me tell you something," the man began. His voice was strong, loud, filled with emotion. "Let me tell you something. I prayed to that God for the first time in my life. I said, 'God, you ain't never been there for me, and you ain't never done anything for me. Everything in my life has been hard. I've been neglected, and I've been abandoned. No one's had my back. I have no hope. If you're real, show me something! If not, I'm going to do anything I can to hurt myself!' And five minutes later you guys show up." And then he broke down again, weeping. In that moment, this man came face to face with the fact that God answers prayer. And God had allowed us to be part of that answer.

I couldn't help but cry. God had a special plan for this young man. And even though at first I didn't feel like walking down this hallway, God had a bigger idea in mind. What mattered most was not how I felt. What mattered was that this man had an appointment to meet Jesus. After we prayed and this man committed his life to God, he looked different. Brighter. His eyes twinkled, full of life. New life.

This man went from darkness to light. From being overwhelmed by despair to full of hope. He may remain behind bars for the rest of his life, but the truth has set him free.

THE TIME IS NOW

God wants us to be a part of awesome things, but we have to say yes to doing something. This means doing something when you feel like it and when you don't, when you're motivated and when you're not. If you have the chance to do the right thing or help brighten someone's day, just do it. Give someone a hug. Invite a friend to church. Tell a teacher how much you appreciate her. Encourage a teammate. Make the new kid in school feel welcome.

One of my favorite sayings is "Oftentimes we don't dream big enough, and oftentimes we don't start small enough." It makes me think of our foundation's annual Night to Shine event. In 2014 we felt led to start this movement. Night to Shine is a nationwide prom centered on God's love for people with special needs ages sixteen and up. We work together with churches around the country to host proms to celebrate and love on these amazing people.

In just its third year, God has grown Night to Shine to three hundred seventy-five churches in the United States and into eleven countries. More than one hundred fifty thousand volunteers all over the world gave seventy-five thousand honored guests an amazing experience.

There was something for everyone to do. Some volunteers acted as buddies. Some simply stood on the red carpet and cheered. Some did hair and makeup. Some stood on a stage and emceed. Some shined shoes. Some parked cars. Some helped decorate. Some helped with the sound system.

Although events like this are great and provide tons of volunteer opportunities, you don't have to wait for a special occasion to serve someone. You can start right now. Look around. Do you know someone who might need some encouragement? Or see someone who might need a hand? Take a step of faith and do something for that person.

Years ago I visited an eleven-year-old boy who had cancer. Though I can't remember why, I was feeling down that day. Despite not feeling particularly motivated, I headed off to spend time with this boy and his family.

When I arrived at their home on a Sunday afternoon, the boy's parents greeted me warmly. We sat down, and they shared their son's story. A tumor had ruptured in his shoulder and shattered it. He was a huge baseball fan and played baseball at his school, and he couldn't use his throwing arm anymore. The boy was heartbroken. My bad day didn't seem so bad anymore.

We talked for a while and prayed some. Our time together was powerful, uplifting. Spending time with this precious boy and his parents changed my perspective. It's interesting what happens when you do something in spite of your feelings. Many times, you walk away being blessed by the one you think you're going to bless. Funny how that works.

> It's interesting what happens when you do something in spite of your feelings.

You know how competitive I am. Winning is everything. When I was playing in the NFL, I trained hard, did my best, and wanted with everything in me to win. But there were times I had to remind myself it was just a game. It's not that it wasn't important. But when millions of Americans are tuning in to watch you perform for the next three hours and the pressure of winning or losing becomes all consuming, you need perspective. I had to remind myself that I was just playing a game, while many others are fighting for their lives.

I got a lot of flak for spending time with W15H kids and others pregame and postgame. I believe these kids helped keep my spirit in the right place. Though I performed just as competitively, most times keeping the right perspective allowed me to handle the pressures of winning and losing better. It helped me not feel like if I didn't score a touchdown, my life would be over.

Here's the thing: society doesn't get to define what's important in my life. Although I may not get a pat on the back or a "Good job!" from others, I'd rather have my heavenly Father be proud of me.

My Heroes

I've been so inspired by our W15H kids and others I've met along the way. Even when they're sick, they help and love on others.

In my first book I talked about Kelly Faughnan, a young woman with a million-dollar smile. I met her in Orlando in 2009. She agreed to be my date to the Home Depot College Football Awards.

Kelly was born with a hearing impairment and severe motor delays. When she was thirteen years old, she started to experience tremors in her right hand and arm. Six months after graduating from high school, doctors discovered a tumor on Kelly's brain stem. A few months later, she underwent brain surgery. The tumor was removed, but the tremors continued. To this day, no one has been able to diagnose Kelly's condition, let alone treat it.

Kelly is amazing. She is a positive and inspirational powerhouse who refuses to let a serious medical condition keep her from enjoying life and making a difference. Oh sure, she has bad days. Sometimes she is embarrassed by the tremors and the way others look at her or say things about her because of them. And sometimes she gets frustrated because she struggles doing even the simplest things—like buttoning her clothes or using a fork and knife. But Kelly fights hard not to let these things bother her. She says with a smile, "My tremors are a part of me. I am the person God made me to be."

After we met for the first time, I kept in touch with her. Two years later she received a W15H. Grateful for the experience, Kelly was inspired to do something herself. She started a golf tournament and an ice-cream-parlor raffle in her hometown and donated all the money to my foundation. Kelly says, "The golf tournament is my way of using the blessings I have been given to create a brighter day in the lives of children who are facing challenges of their own." The event was so successful that Kelly has organized one every year. So far she has raised eighty-five thousand dollars.

Incredible!

I was a senior in college, playing my last year of football as a Gator, when I met seven-year-old Boomer, an adorable kid with a mischievous smile. Boomer was born three months early at twenty-eight weeks. When he was just over a year old, he was diagnosed with schizencephaly, a developmental birth defect, and cerebral palsy (like

Robyn in chapter 7). Doctors said he would never sit up, never walk, and not make it past age five. But, despite the physical challenges and the pain he has, Boomer beat the odds.

Boomer and his mom drove down to Florida from Atlanta to meet me for the first time before the Gators opened the season. I had a blast wheeling this incredible kid (and huge Gator fan) around the field for warmups before the game and in between the maze of benches in the locker room. We stayed in touch after that, sending each other encouraging texts.

The first year we held the foundation's Celebrity Golf Classic, we did our best to fill the room with a bunch of supporters and donors who could help our cause. Planning this event took a ton of work and time. Our staff was small and put in countless hours of work.

The event started with a prayer, led by none other than Boomer, who was there with his mother. In a ballroom decked out with fancy tableware and shiny chandeliers, this amazing kid, looking stylish in a three-piece suit and tie, rolled up to the front of the podium in his wheelchair. After he led the room in a moving opening prayer, he did something astonishing.

> **After he led the room in a moving opening prayer, he did something astonishing.**

As Boomer left the stage, he handed me a clear Ziploc bag. Inside were a few crumpled dollar bills and a bunch of loose change. Twenty-seven dollars in total. On the bag written in blue ink was "To Timmy's foundation, From Boomer."

"I saved this from my allowance," he said, beaming. "I want to help. I want to give it to you." I choked back a tear as I leaned down and took the plastic bag from him. The change jiggled wildly. Still on stage, I shared with all these wealthy and influential people Boomer's act of generosity. The supporters of the foundation were in tears, moved by the inspiring act of a little boy who chose to do something. And many of them were inspired to give as well.

Do something. Trust me, it counts.

The next year, Boomer surprised us again. In our second golf event, he presented us with checks totaling $9,267. Every single person in that room started crying, as most had attended the event the year before and remembered Boomer. It was a powerful and emotional moment. And, once again, it led others to give, too.

Maybe you shy away from reaching out and helping others because you're scared your efforts won't matter or won't make much of a difference. Have courage and at least try. You don't know what God can do with one step forward, with a raised hand, with a heart that says yes, with five loaves and two fish, with a slingshot and a few stones, with twenty-seven dollars. Don't limit what He can do based on how you limit yourself. Be yourself, and let God be God. When you know whose you are, you can live in a way that makes a lasting difference.

10

WHAT MATTERS MOST

There is so much more to our existence
than what we can see. What we do reverberates
through the heavens and into eternity.

—Francis Chan

Eleven seconds. What can you do in eleven seconds? Wash your hands. Send a text. Tie your shoes. Google something. Download an app.

Meb Keflezighi won the 2014 Boston Marathon by eleven seconds.

And eleven seconds into overtime, the Denver Broncos knocked the Pittsburgh Steelers, the number one defense in the NFL at the time, out of the AFC playoffs, 29–23.

It was a chilly day in Denver on January 8, 2012. As I warmed up pregame, it was hard to shake the disappointment from losing the last three games against the Patriots, the Buffalo Bills, and the Kansas City Chiefs. The losses were painful. Especially because we'd just celebrated a six-week winning streak before that. This included six fourth-quarter comebacks against Oakland, Kansas City, the New York Jets, San Diego, Minnesota, and Chicago.

The media had a field day with our recent losses. After losing

14–40 to Buffalo, one news commentator took to Twitter with a blow against my faith, using a ton of profanity. On Christmas Eve, no less. Others in the media asked where God was during our three-week slump.

I'll admit, my performances weren't great. During those last three games I completed only 41 percent of my passes. I hated seeing how the public blamed God for the losses. Hey, I never said He was responsible for our wins or our crazy comebacks. I just thanked Him in those moments.

So on that chilly January day, taking the field in practice, warming up with my fellow teammates prior to facing the Steelers, it was hard not to think about our last three games.

I reminded myself of the psalms I had been studying recently. Much of this collection of prayers and poems was written by David, a king of ancient Israel, the warrior boy who took out the giant. I brought to mind Psalm 16:8: "I have set the LORD continually before me; because He is at my right hand, I will not be shaken." I remembered when I was a sophomore in high school, quarterback of our football team. Every Friday night before games, my parents would always encourage me with Bible verses. After my mom read Psalm 16:8 to me, I asked her for a black Sharpie. Then I scribbled something on my hand. Mom assumed I was writing down a play or something.

After we won the game, she asked, "Honey, what did you write on your hand?" I opened my palm with a smile. Though the mixture of sweat and dirt had smudged some of the letters, on my right hand in faint black was the word *God*.

That afternoon in Denver, I set my mind on Psalm 16:8. I reminded myself that God was at my right hand. I chose to praise and thank Him. I would have loved a win, of course. But no matter the outcome, I made the choice to keep trusting and thanking my heavenly Father.

Before the game, I was honored to be able to hang out with Bailey, one of our W15H kids. Diagnosed with a rare disease that forms tumors in the face, lungs, and kidneys, Bailey's had seventy-five surgeries so far. Despite her medical battle, this girl is on fire. I'll never forget how encouraging she was to me. As the stadium started filling with football fans, she kept telling me, "Relax, Timmy! I'm praying for you. You're going to do awesome!" It's amazing how Bailey helped put the game into perspective. By the time our team lined up on the opening snap and seventy-six thousand football fans started screaming, I was ready.

> I made the choice to keep trusting and thanking my heavenly Father.

The first quarter wasn't great. Our Broncos offense managed only eight yards, with no passes completed on my part. But in the second quarter, we pulled the trigger. After hitting Eric Decker and Demaryius Thomas on a few big plays, we got the ball rolling. At halftime, the Broncos were up 20–6.

Our lead didn't last long. The Steelers came on strong in the second half, scoring on three straight possessions. And with 3:48 remaining in the game, they knotted the score 23–23 with a thirty-one-yard touchdown pass. The game ended in a tie.

Pittsburgh called tails for the overtime coin toss. The shiny penny (or whatever it was) landed heads up on the grass.

I didn't know how long it would take, but I knew the play we'd make. We talked about it on the sidelines. And in watching how the Steelers had played the game, it seemed a perfect fit. Their team had an aggressive defense and had been trying to stop our zone-read. This one play, I thought, just might be our golden ticket.

After the refs explained the NFL's new overtime rules, we set up on the 20-yard line. When the ball snapped, my confidence grew. *We might have a chance with this play.* When Thomas did a great job getting inside the corner, crossing in front of the safety, I knew we definitely had a chance.

I faked to halfback Willis McGahee and threw to a streaking Thomas. As we hoped, the Steelers overreacted on the play and gave Thomas the room he needed to catch the pass and take off down the sideline. Past the fifty. To the forty. Past the thirty. To the twenty, with Steelers safety Ryan Mundy chasing behind, his arms outstretched trying to grab Thomas as he whizzed forward like a speeding bullet. And eleven seconds after the ball was snapped, touchdown!

Mile High Stadium was delirious. Broncos fans jumped up and down, whooping and hollering. Steelers fans slowly disappeared from the stands one by one. This eleven-second play, to date known as the fastest overtime win in the history of the NFL, invited a wild celebration across the field. Swept up in the uproar, I took a knee on the gridiron, said a prayer, gave a mile-high salute, and celebrated with my teammates. Drowning in a sea of blue and orange, we hugged and high-fived, practically falling all over one another. It's a moment I'll never forget.

Mile High Stadium was delirious.

This was the same game our publicity guy said I threw for 316 yards, my yards per completion was 31.6, the time of possession was 31:06, the ratings were 31.6 million. And during the game ninety million people Googled "John 3:16"!

That day is one of the most memorable moments in my life. And while I appreciate the record-breaking scene as a highlight in my career, I know records are made to be broken. There will always be someone else to win next year's title, award, or trophy. These things don't last.

I want my life to speak louder than a world record. I don't just want to leave a legacy on the field. I want to live in a way that outlives me. I want my love for God and for others to take center stage.

WHO IS THE GREATEST?

A few months after I won the Heisman in my sophomore year of college, I was invited to Thailand to speak to hundreds of missionaries serving in South Asia, including my sister Christy and her husband,

Joey, who had moved to the region to serve. As I flew overseas, excited about the opportunity, I was also pretty nervous. What was a twenty-year-old college kid going to share with a bunch of missionaries who were risking their very lives for the message of Jesus? I couldn't stop thinking things like, *I'm not a pastor or Bible teacher. I'm not a missionary like my dad or Christy or Joey. I didn't even go to Bible school! What on earth am I going to say?*

I wondered why I was even asked to speak. These missionaries were heroes. They could teach me a thing or two. At the time I was getting a lot of attention as a college ballplayer, especially after winning the Heisman. I stared out the window of the plane as it flew over the Pacific Ocean. The sky beamed blue, the sun blasting my eyes. I wondered, *If I lived in a world that didn't have football, who would I be? Would I still matter?* The more I struggled to figure out what to share, the smaller I felt. Then I felt God reminding me of one of the Bible verses my parents forced me to memorize when teaching me about humility.

> But the greatest among you shall be your servant. Whoever exalts himself shall be humbled; and whoever humbles himself shall be exalted. (Matthew 23:11–12)

Later, I stood before hundreds of men and women and encouraged them from my heart. Using this verse, I told them that while some might look at movie stars or politicians or athletes as heroes, the real heroes are those who are humble. And because they had chosen to humble themselves and serve people that some may consider "the least of these,"[1] God lifts them up. As I finished my talk, I told these incredible missionaries that if the world could see them through God's eyes, they would be the ones winning the Heisman, not me.

I admire missionaries like Dad, Mom, Christy, and Joey because they are investing in others in ways that will last for eternity. Who we are has to be bigger than what we have. Than what we look like. Than where we live. Than who we know. When we are secure in our identity, we can live with purpose. And when we live with purpose, we can leave a lasting impact on others and on this world. You don't need to be a missionary to do this. Share the Good News of Jesus. Encourage a stranger. Use the talent God has given you. Take a stand. Do the right thing, even when it's hard.

THE DIFFERENCE ONE CHOICE CAN MAKE

A few years back I spoke at an event where I shared the message of God's hope and love with thousands of people. After I ended my message and the emcee took over to close, I started walking toward the side of the stage. I didn't get too far before I heard a loud female voice calling my name. I turned to the audience that was starting to pack up and leave, and I noticed a young woman in her twenties. Tears streamed down her face as she ran toward me. I wasn't the only one who saw her. Part of the event security team was nearby. One rushed to block me with his huge arms and another moved toward the woman to keep her from getting too close. But she was persistent. She kept trying to get my attention.

Suddenly, an older woman, also crying, rushed toward the young woman. She was holding a baby in her arms. By this point, I was curious. What on earth did they want? I took a few steps toward these two women. Security did the same. The older woman handed the baby off to the younger one, who was still calling out my name. She took the child and lifted her high in the air. I motioned for security to back off a bit so I could talk to her.

The young lady seemed relieved. She managed to blurt out in between sniffles and sobs, "I just want you to hold a life that you helped save." Then she mentioned the TV commercial my mom and I had recently done in 2010. The message of the thirty-second clip was simple: Celebrate family. Celebrate life.

This young woman had visited the website that shared my mom's story. She learned that when my mom became pregnant with me in the Philippines, she was very sick. The medications given to her had likely damaged me in the womb. In fact, the best doctor where they lived described me as a mass of fetal tissue. He advised my mom to end the pregnancy by having an abortion (a medical procedure that terminates the life of an unborn child) in order to save her own life. She refused, trusting God with the outcome of my life and hers. While she was physically ill the entire time she was pregnant with me, Mom's faith was strong. She was confident God was in control.

You know how that story ends.

Years later, sitting with this young woman in an auditorium, I listened as she said, "A few days after the commercial aired, I was scheduled to have an abortion." Tears streamed down her face as she looked lovingly at her baby. "But I didn't."

What a powerful moment. I can remember the handful of people who suggested I not do the commercial. Some said it was a bad idea because it would influence some of my sponsors to back out of their deals with me. But because I am passionate about celebrating life, I thought the commercial was brilliant. And I was honored to be a part of it.

> Because I am passionate about celebrating life, I thought the commercial was brilliant.

I believe that every life matters. No matter how big or little, no matter the race or nationality, no matter the disability or not, no matter if it's in the womb or fixing to go into the grave, every single life counts.

I admire Mom more than words can say for the legacy she is leaving her family, a legacy of courage, of standing strong, and of always doing the right thing. It is my hope that one day my own children will say the same of me.

YOUR LIFE ECHOES

I love the film *Gladiator*. In the opening battle scene, the Roman general Maximus rides a majestic horse through thousands of soldiers who are prepared to fight. He gives a powerful speech and tells these men, "What we do in life echoes in eternity."

I love these words. They remind me how important it is to live bigger. To do things in life that matter in the big picture. To set our minds on things that last.

Think about your life. How are you spending your time? Your talents? Are you sharing hope? Are you loving others? Are you taking a stand? Doing something that matters?

Not long ago, I was thinking about my goals and what I want to accomplish. I do this often. It reminds me of what's important and helps me decide how and where I will spend my time. With a marker in hand, I stood in front of a giant whiteboard. I started jotting down ideas. *Write another book. Take a mission trip to the Philippines.* I noticed a recurring theme. That day I realized that my number one goal in life is to show Jesus through the way I live and the way I love. This doesn't mean I always do it right. This doesn't mean I always do it the best way. But all in all, it's something I strive for.

When we think about living bigger, it comes down to letting Jesus shine through us. In what we say, how we act, how we lead, how we serve, how we talk to one another, where we invest our time, what we do with our talents.

I love 2 Corinthians 4:17–18: "For our present troubles are small and won't last very long. Yet they produce for us a glory that vastly outweighs them and will last forever! So we don't look at the troubles we can see now; rather, we fix our gaze on things that cannot be seen. For the things we see now will soon be gone, but the things we cannot see will last forever" (NLT). Trophies don't last. Awards come and go. Money and social media followers, too. But how we live can make an eternal difference.

For the last two years or so, I've been friends with a girl named Ansley Jones. I met her at Wolfson Children's Hospital in November 2013 when she was fourteen. This sweet and strong girl was diagnosed with leukemia a month before and was going through chemotherapy treatment. Ansley, whom I call "my southern girl," happens to be the nicest Georgia Bulldogs fan, and she is also one of the most posi-

> **Despite being sick, she is always smiling, laughing, and making jokes.**

tive people I know. Despite being sick, she is always smiling, laughing, and making jokes. Ansley has a way of making people around her light up. In fact, she's known for visiting and encouraging other kids in the hospital who are just as sick as she is.

As I was working on this book, Ansley was in the hospital recovering from a pretty serious procedure. Every time I visited, I'd sit next to her and we'd talk and pray. Oh, and have a blast creating a ton of Dubsmash videos with songs like "A Whole New World" and the soundtrack from *Grease*.

Ansley takes kindness to a whole new level. No matter how sick or tired she is, she is always so thoughtful and nice to everyone around her. Honestly, she makes me want to treat people better. It's easy to be kind to others when you're feeling great, but it takes strength to do it when you're not feeling very well. Ansley's life speaks to many people, me especially, through her courage to fight and her caring spirit.

Think about what your life says to others. Are you living in a way that is centered on yourself? Or are you, like Ansley, living in a way that helps others?

WELL DONE

I've talked a lot about investing in others because it's a big part of our identity in Jesus. When we know whose we are, we live differently. We're not the same. Our outlook changes. We understand that some things we do on earth will last for eternity.

At the end of my life, it doesn't matter how much praise or how many pats on the back I've gotten from others. What I really want to hear is my heavenly Father tell me, "I'm proud of you, son" (my translation of the Bible's "Well done, my good and faithful servant"[2]).

You know that John 3:16 is the heart of Christianity. It tells us that God loved the world so much that He willingly gave His only Son, Jesus. He did this so that we could be free from sin and live an abundant life. This is the Good News. In fact, it's the best news.

The ultimate legacy we can leave behind is a life of faith, believing the gospel and living in a way that honors Jesus.

Two thousand years ago, a baby was born who would change the world. The Son of God left heaven to come down to earth to die for the sins of all people. Jesus gave up everything He had for me. For you. It seems crazy when you really think about it. On a dirt floor caked with mud, scattered with rough straw that baaing sheep and mooing cows trample on, Jesus is born. The scene isn't pretty. It's not a hospital room with a soft bed and clean sheets. God takes on human flesh in a dirty manger.

And for thirty-three years, Jesus walks on earth. He takes His first steps as a baby. He skips stones on lakes. He horses around with the neighborhood kids. As He grows up, Jesus works alongside His dad, a carpenter.

At just the right time, Jesus begins His public ministry. He gets baptized. And then He starts sharing the Good News. He heals people. He gives them peace. He offers forgiveness. Not everyone likes Jesus. The religious leaders want him dead. And so these men plot to kill Him. Jesus dies for us on a cross. In that moment, the weight of sin was upon Him. My sin. And your sin. And during that time, Jesus was separated from God the Father. He was rejected so we don't have to be. He was abandoned so we don't have to be.

But this redemption story doesn't stop there. On the third day after He died, Jesus rose from the dead. He's alive!

What people planned for evil, God planned for good. Through His death and resurrection, Jesus gives us new life. We can actually have a relationship with the Creator of the universe. And it's free! We can't earn our salvation. We can't do enough good deeds. In fact, even our best efforts are not enough to deserve it. We receive it only by trusting Jesus.

The Most Important Decision

When I think about living a life that matters, I think about a big perspective—eternity. I think about making decisions that will honor God. I believe the greatest legacy we can leave is a life lived for Jesus. That starts with the most important decision you will ever make: the decision to trust Him. This is the best decision I ever made.

If you have never asked Jesus into your heart, I want to encourage you to do it right now with your mom or dad or even on your own. You can use your own words or read mine here:

> Dear Jesus, I know I am a sinner and need a Savior. Thank You that You died for me and rose again from the dead. I open the door of my heart and ask You to come in. Thank You for coming into my heart and forgiving my sins. Thank You that God is my Father and I am His child. Thank You that I have a home in heaven and that I will come and live with You someday. In Your name, amen.

If you just prayed that prayer, here are a few awesome things to know. Your sins are forgiven. Jesus lives in you. You are adopted into God's family as one of His children. And you have the free gift of eternal life. Because this life you have in Jesus is everlasting, He will never leave you or forsake you.[3]

No matter what happens in life—good or bad—God offers you

a new life. A life of meaning. A life of purpose. A life of joy. Yes, even when life hurts.

The journey of faith isn't easy. Life isn't easy. But when you are united to Jesus by faith, you can begin to move mountains. Listen, you're going to doubt. You're going to fall short. You're going to struggle some days. But know that God loves you. Know that He has an amazing plan for your life. And even when bad times come, it's worth it. When you make the choice to show up and show out for Jesus, He will show up and show out for you.

Know this: you are not defined by the highs in life or the lows. From this day forward, let God define who you are.

Continue to fight. Continue to hope. Continue to have faith.

I promise you, it's worth it.

Acknowledgments

Dad, you are the greatest man I know, with unmatched passion and courage. Through your devotion, commitment, and obedience to the Great Commission, you have changed countless lives for Jesus. Thank you for setting the example.

Mom, thank you! For everything! For giving me a chance, for always believing in me and my siblings, for pouring God's Word into our lives, for always wanting what's best for us, and for helping so many women all over the world along the way. If we've achieved anything, you're the reason why.

Christy, you're the best role model. Your wisdom and discernment have been such a blessing to me, especially through our late-night talks. Being able to watch you live out your faith in the highs and lows has been a true inspiration. Thank you for always being there for me.

Joey, you have blessed our family in more ways than you can imagine. Thank you for all the godly wisdom you've offered over the years, and especially on this project, and also for taking care of my sister. You're more than a brother-in-law; you are my brother.

Katie, you are a pillar of courage and inspiration. Thank you for how much you care and for always putting a smile on my face. You bring so much life and spirit into my life and everyone around you. It's never a party if you're not there.

Robby, thank you for sticking by my side through thick and thin and for always having my back. We've been through a lot of highs and lows together, and there's no one else I'd rather have been with. You can have my rookie of DiMaggio.

Peter, I've always loved your heart and your tenacity. You're a fighter, and when you set your mind to something, nothing can stop you. I've loved watching you grow from brother to husband to father. Little Jackson is blessed to have you and Casey as parents!

Kevin, thank you for always being loyal and for being there for me since we were four years old.

Bryan, you know you're family and you'll always be. I'm excited to continue to do life with you.

Brad, thank you for bringing so much joy into my life. I'm so proud of what God is doing in yours.

Erik, thank you for being a great Christian brother and for the leadership and vision you have brought to the Tim Tebow Foundation (TTF).

To the staff and volunteers of TTF, thank you for the passion and dedication you bring to *our* foundation and the children we serve around the world.

To all the families and children we serve through TTF, thank you for allowing me to be part of your life! You have encouraged and inspired me by your amazing lives and stories.

Wendy, you are so much more than my attorney; you are family. Thank you for everything.

Annie, thank you for making the ship run smoothly—and always with a smile.

Ian, thank you for your friendship and wisdom.

AJ, you crushed it! From your incredible patience, talent, and class to your love of the Lord, I wouldn't want anyone else helping me share my story.

The Fedd Agency: Whitney and Esther, thank you for believing in this project and for your tireless devotion.

The team at WaterBrook (Tina, Alex, Laura B., Bruce, Laura W.): thank you for the insight and support you lent to this project.

To everyone who has ever prayed for me, thank you.

Notes

Chapter 2: Who Am I?

1. "The Unconditional Love of God," Bible Study Tools, September 13, 2012, www.biblestudytools.com/bible-study/topical -studies/the-unconditional-love-of-god.html.
2. 1 John 4:16.
3. Audio Adrenaline, *Hands and Feet* (Regal, 2007), back cover.
4. "Among Jordan's Great Games, This Was It," *Los Angeles Times,* March 29, 1990, http://articles.latimes.com/1990-03-29 /sports/sp-582_1_michael-jordan.
5. See John 6:5.
6. John 6:10, NLT.

Chapter 3: Facing the Giants

1. "Tim Tebow Leads 2-TD Rally as Broncos Stun Winless Dolphins in OT," ESPN.com News Service, October 24, 2011, http://espn.go.com/nfl/recap?gameId=311023015; Gray Caldwell, "The Comeback," Denver Broncos, October 23, 2011, www.denverbroncos.com/news-and-blogs/article-1/The -Comeback/cf2a853e-75d2-49ef-a497-b9344631cb92.
2. Luke 22:42.
3. Luke 22:42.

4. Janet St. James, "North Texas 20-Year-Old Fights for Life Against Cancer," WFAA, September 5, 2014, www.cincinnati.com/story/news/state/2014/09/06/north-texas-20-year-old-fights-for-life-against-cancer/15209841.

5. See 2 Timothy 4:7, NIV.

6. Hebrews 11:1.

7. Martin Luther King Jr., quoted in Joseph Demakis, *The Ultimate Book of Quotations* (Charleston, SC: CreateSpace, 2012), 142.

8. "David and Goliath," All About the Bible, www.allaboutthebible.net/warfare/david-and-goliath.

9. 1 Samuel 17:8–10, NIV.

10. See 1 Samuel 17:18.

11. See 1 Samuel 17:20–26.

12. 1 Samuel 17:43, NIV.

13. 1 Samuel 17:45–46, NIV.

Chapter 4: The Voices of Negativity

1. Mark Kiszla, "Broncos Need New Meaning for Tim Tebowing," *Denver Post,* October 30, 2011, www.denverpost.com/broncos/ci_19228711.

2. Bruce Arthur, "Tebowing Mocking Enters Dangerous Territory," *National Post,* November 2, 2011, http://news.nationalpost.com/sports/nfl/tim-tebow-mocking-enters-dangerous-territory.

Chapter 5: God's Got It

1. "Eagles Release QB Tim Tebow," ESPN.com News Service, September 6, 2015, http://espn.go.com/nfl/story/_/id /13588372/tim-tebow-released-philadelphia-eagles.

2. Job 1:8, MSG.

3. See Job 1:9–10.

4. See Job 1:11.

5. See Job 2:9.

6. Job 13:15.

7. See Job 38–39.

8. John 16:33, NLT.

9. Gary White, "Mulberry Teen Gets a Second Heart Transplant," *Ledger* (Lakeland, FL), March 12, 2013, www.theledger.com /article/20130312/NEWS/130319797?p=2&tc=pg.

10. Romans 8:28.

11. 1 Corinthians 13:12.

Chapter 6: The Others

1. Ecclesiastes 4:12, NLT.

2. Proverbs 18:24.

3. David DiSalvo, "Study: Helping Others Even in Small Ways Takes the Edge off Daily Stress," *Forbes,* December 21, 2015, www.forbes.com/sites/daviddisalvo/2015/12/21/helping-others -even-in-small-ways-takes-the-edge-off-daily-stress/#2a0b9aa 35136.

4. Blago Kirov, *Ralph Waldo Emerson: Quotes and Facts* (Charleston, SC: CreateSpace, 2016), 38.

Chapter 7: Who Said Normal Is the Goal?

1. "What Is Cerebral Palsy?" www.handi-capable.org/templates /handi/site/archives/What%20is%20CP.pdf.
2. 1 Peter 4:10, NLT.
3. 1 Corinthians 4:7.

Chapter 8: Stand Up

1. Tom Weir, "'Tebowing' Becomes Officially Recognized as a Word," *USA Today*, December 12, 2011, http://content.usa today.com/communities/gameon/post/2011/12/tim-tebow -tebowing-officially-recognized-as-a-word/1#.WVKvzesrKUk.
2. See http://tebowing.com/about.
3. Simon Paige, *The Very Best of Winston Churchill: Quotes from a British Legend* (Charleston, SC: CreateSpace, 2014), 15.

Chapter 9: The Power of Doing Something

1. 2 Timothy 3:16, NLT.

Chapter 10: What Matters Most

1. Matthew 25:40, 45, NIV.
2. Matthew 25:23, NLT.
3. See Hebrews 13:5, NIV.

About the Author

Tim Tebow is a two-time national champion, first-round NFL draft pick, and Heisman Trophy winner. After playing in the NFL for the Denver Broncos and the New York Jets, Tebow joined the SEC Network. In addition to his role on *SEC Nation,* the network's traveling road show, Tebow also contributes to a variety of other ESPN platforms. In 2016, he signed a professional baseball contract with the New York Mets. Through everything, Tim's true passion remains the work of the Tim Tebow Foundation, which he began in 2010. The foundation's mission is to bring Faith, Hope, and Love to those needing a brighter day in their darkest hour of need. The foundation is fulfilling that mission every day by serving thousands of deserving children around the world.

TIM TEBOW
FOUNDATION™

FAITH • HOPE • LOVE

To continue to fight for those who can't fight for themselves, a portion of proceeds from each book sold will be donated to the **Tim Tebow Foundation** to help further their mission of:

Bringing Faith, Hope and Love to those needing a brighter day in their darkest hour of need.

The foundation is currently fulfilling this mission every day by...

- Providing life-changing surgeries through the **Tebow CURE Hospital** to children of the Philippines who could not otherwise afford care.

- Creating a worldwide movement through **Night to Shine**, an unforgettable prom experience, centered on God's love, for people with special needs.

- Building **Timmy's Playrooms** in children's hospitals around the world.

- Fulfilling the dreams of children with life-threatening illnesses through the **W15H** program.

- Encouraging volunteer service to others through **Team Tebow** and **Team Tebow Kids**.

- Supporting housing, meals, medical treatment and education for orphans around the world though our **Orphan Care** program.

- Providing **Adoption Aid** financial assistance to families who are making the courageous choice to adopt a child with special needs internationally.

...simply put, Serving Children and Sharing God's Love!

To learn more about these initiatives and the continued growth of the foundation's outreach ministries, visit **www.timtebowfoundation.org.**

ADDITIONAL RESOURCES

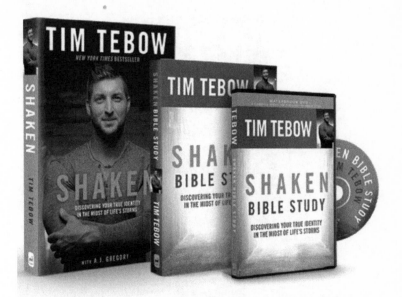

What defines your self-worth? Is it your successes or your failures? Former NFL quarterback, Tim Tebow, shares never-before-told details about his joys and disappointments on and off the field. With captivating honesty, Tebow explains how his identity has remained steadfast and secured in God alone.

WATERBROOK

THE ONLY IDENTITY WORTH HAVING...
IS FOUND IN JESUS CHRIST

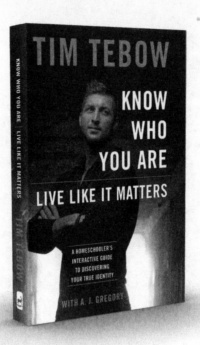

American sports icon Tim Tebow knows firsthand what it's like to face pressure head-on. In *Know Who You Are. Live Like It Matters,* he shares the wisdom he's learned—not from what the world says, but from what God says in His word. Tim will guide you through thirty-six weeks of lessons, each based on a key Scripture, to discover who you are—by learning more about whose you are!